Beyond Liberation Theology

Other books by Humberto Belli:

Nicaragua: Christians under Fire
Breaking Faith

Other books by Ronald H. Nash:

Worldviews in Conflict
Great Divides
Poverty and Wealth
The Word of God and the Mind of Man
The Gospel and the Greeks
The Closing of the American Heart
Choosing a College
Faith and Reason
Social Justice and the Christian Church
Process Theology (editor)
Liberation Theology (editor)
Evangelical Renewal in the Mainline Churches (editor)
Christian Faith and Historical Understanding
The Concept of God
Evangelicals in America
Freedom, Justice and the State
The Light of the Mind
Ideas of History (editor)
The Case for Biblical Christianity (editor)
The Philosophy of Gordon H. Clark (editor)
The New Evangelicalism
Dooyeweerd and the Amsterdam Philosophy

Beyond Liberation Theology

Humberto Belli
and
Ronald H. Nash

BAKER BOOK HOUSE
Grand Rapids, Michigan 49516

Library of Congress Cataloging-in-Publication Data

Belli, Humberto.
    Beyond liberation theology / Humberto Belli and Ronald Nash.
        p.   cm.
    Includes bibliographical references and index.
    ISBN 0-8010-1022-5
    1. Liberation theology. 2. Communism and Christianity. 3. Capitalism—
religious aspects—Christianity. I. Nash, Ronald H. II. Title.
BT83.57.B45   1992
261.7—dc20   92-15728

Contents

Preface

The essential claims of this book are two. The first is a descriptive claim for which we intend to show that there is already ample empirical support: that liberation theology in the 1990s is changing so dramatically that many of its proponents will soon believe things utterly contradictory to the earlier movement's most important and prominent beliefs. The second is a normative claim for which we hope to give ample support: that these changes are praiseworthy. Indeed, we go even further. We argue that the older, earlier versions of liberation theology were mistaken from the beginning. The shape of the new liberation theology, which is becoming more apparent with every passing day, includes views that never should have been omitted from any viable liberation theology.

In 1987, Richard John Neuhaus wrote that some interpreters dared to suggest that liberation theology had become a "failed and fading experiment."[1] While at the time Neuhaus was unsure where he stood on the question, he was confident nonetheless that liberation theology had changed significantly since its infancy in the 1960s. He went on to speculate about still future changes that would be so dramatic that possibly only the name *liberation theology* would remain.[2]

---

1. Richard John Neuhaus, *The Catholic Moment* (San Francisco: Harper and Row, 1987), 171.
2. Ibid., 172.

George Weigel, president of the Ethics and Public Policy Center in Washington, D.C., had the same topic in mind when he wrote, "There is considerable talk these days, that liberation theology may be passing into a second phase: less wedded to Marxist analysis, more concerned about democracy and the possibilities of the market, deeper in its spirituality and considerably less adolescent in its politics. That would be a welcome development."[3]

While library and bookstore shelves groan under the enormous weight of the hundreds of books, most supportive, that the liberation movement has begotten, this book is the first to take seriously the suggestions that liberationism either has entered its inevitable period of decline or is undergoing a metamorphosis so dramatic that in the end it will be a wholly new movement. Indeed, we have argued for years on behalf of a *new* liberation theology.[4] We are reassured to see the tide finally moving in directions we have recommended.

If the old liberation theology ought to change, some have asked, why not also abandon the label? Given the heavy burden the term *liberation theology* carries because of its past connotations, the suggestion has merit. But there is also good reason to retain the word *liberation*. As later sections of this book will argue, no religion in the history of the world has been more concerned with providing human beings with genuine liberation than Christianity.

Beyond Liberation Theology is the first book to challenge the monopoly earlier versions of liberationism have had on the liberation label. It is the first book to argue *explicitly*[5] that it is time

3. George Weigel, "A New Opiate: Liberation Theology," *Insight*, March 2, 1987, 69.

4. Others who contributed to this important task include a company of Catholic scholars like Michael Novak, George Weigel, and Richard John Neuhaus. As later sections of this book will argue, this has also been a major burden of Pope John Paul II.

5. The list of books arguing implicitly for this thesis would have to include at least the following: Ronald H. Nash, *Poverty and Wealth: Why Socialism Has Failed* (Richardson, Tex.: Probe, 1992 [1st ed., 1986]); Ronald H. Nash, *Social Justice and the Christian Church* (Lanham, Md.: University Press of America, 1992 [1st ed., 1983]); Ronald H. Nash, ed., *Liberation Theology* (Grand Rapids: Baker, 1988); and Michael Novak, *Will It Liberate? Questions about Liberation Theology* (Mahwah, N.J.: Paulist, 1986). The list should also include the Vatican statements on liberation theology that appeared in 1984, 1986, 1988, and 1991.

to move beyond the liberation theology of the past and begin to formulate new and more adequate means of dealing with the human need for liberation from poverty, oppression, and sin. Whatever the efforts recommended in this book come to be called by future generations, what now seems irrefutable is that earlier, older versions of liberation theology never were what the world needed and that only time and changing circumstances were needed to make this clear.

What finally toppled the liberation apple cart? The unforeseen and utterly incredible events that some now call "the revolutions of 1989." The sudden, sweeping changes that affected Eastern Europe and now have stabbed deeply into the heart of Soviet life and thought have unveiled once and for all what many economists and philosophers had argued for years: the bankruptcy of socialism. It has helped neither the reputation nor the morale of advocates of the old liberation theology that the revolutions of 1989 repudiated the very ideas they held dear.

Some better-known Latin American liberationists now are distancing themselves from former beliefs and embracing, however tentatively and ruefully, an idea once unthinkable: that capitalism just might have something to offer the world's poor after all. North American liberationists, however, are more intractable in their fanatical attachment to socialism. Those who dominate the mainline Protestant denominations and many seminaries and college religion departments in the U.S. are not especially happy these days. They and their institutions may very well be the last vestiges of the older, now discredited liberation theology. No doubt one reason for this is the extent to which North American liberationists have made liberationism part of a broader package that includes all the causes integral to the *Zeitgeist* of the radical Left.

We agree that the Christian church should pay serious attention to the social dimensions of the Christian gospel. It should be concerned with poverty and oppression; it should become an advocate of the poor; it should seek ways in which poor and non-poor alike can attain genuine liberation. But we also insist on a clear distinction between means and ends. It is one thing to have a noble end, like helping people attain liberation from poverty. But it is even more important that this worthwhile end be linked to means that really will achieve it.

Much liberation theology of the older type supported means that were counterproductive because they impeded genuine and lasting progress toward the desired goals. The more radical liberation thinkers understood little of how the poor may be delivered from economic oppression. They were disturbingly complacent about democracy. And many were noticeably lax about understanding and interpreting how the Christian faith deals with the most important kind of liberation of all, liberation from sin. Our title, *Beyond Liberation Theology*, reflects our conviction that it is time to craft a liberation theology that is both more faithful to the essential theological concerns of historic Christianity and more promising as a means of genuine liberation from poverty and tyranny. We seek the form and content of a true liberation theology.

This book should be useful in several ways. It is a readable introduction to one of the most widely discussed movements of our generation. But, as is already clear, it is a critical introduction; unlike most books on the subject, it is no slavish servant of liberation ideas. It also can be used as a textbook for college and seminary courses that examine the liberation movement. The book places liberation thought in its historical, theological, philosophical, and social setting. Readers will become familiar with the major steps in the origin and development of liberation theology. They will learn the names and views of major liberation thinkers and come to understand why so many scholars have found earlier formulations of liberationism inadequate. They will also come to appreciate why legitimate liberation concerns and insights need to be preserved, even while the church develops a new and more adequate theology of liberation.

The idea for this book arose several years ago over lunch in Virginia Beach, Virginia. At the time, Humberto Belli was an exile from his native Nicaragua, president of the Puebla Institute, and about to begin a tenure as a professor of sociology at the Franciscan University of Steubenville. Ron Nash was a professor of philosophy and religion at a large midwestern state university. Both had published and lectured widely on liberation theology. Now that the book is complete, the situation in the world is dramatically different. Belli is Minister of Education in democratic Nicaragua, where his tasks include shaping the future of education in Nicaragua and helping his homeland cultivate the political, economic, and religious liberties denied it in the past. Nash has retired from his university position and is now a professor of philosophy and theology at Reformed Theological Seminary in Orlando, Florida. Much of his future work helping people achieve liberation will be directed toward Eastern Europe and the nations that, as we write, still make up elements of the old Soviet empire. What has been occurring in these nations is a much richer example of a true liberation theology than anything the old liberation theologians ever accomplished or even approached in their finest dreams.

Introduction

During the summer of 1991, one author of this book was busy serving as Minister of Education in democratic, post-Sandinista Nicaragua, trying to remedy the ravages of years of unjust rule by both Right-wing and Left-wing tyrannies. The other was part of a team of Americans in the Soviet Union as guests of the Ministry of Education of the Russian Republic. While there, he witnessed the astounding changes occurring in Russia that shortly gave birth to the extraordinary events of August 1991 when the Soviet people resoundingly renounced communism. Now, as this chapter is being written, communism is being eradicated from its homeland, the Soviet Union, and from the evil men and ideas that gave it life.

While Humberto Belli plays a central role in steering Nicaragua toward the new liberation theology discussed in this book, Ron Nash works with a team helping democratic and reform-minded Soviets pursue a liberation theology that can guide them out of the labyrinth of Marxism.

The old liberation theology, as we call it, never envisioned anything remotely like either of these tasks. Many early liberation theologians intended to help poor nations in the Third World achieve liberation from "capitalist imperialism," which supposedly caused and perpetuated their poverty. They thought liberation theology would move those nations toward some version of the socialism modelled in the Soviet Union, communist China, Eastern European countries, and Cuba. Some liberationists perfunctorily criticized this or that feature of Soviet or Chinese Marxism when pressed, but none protested Fidel Castro's totalitarianism, and several as we shall see showered shameful adulation on some of this century's worst tyrants.

A few weeks before the Russian revolution of August 1991, Ron Nash stood in the anteroom to the president's office at a prominent Moscow college. Glancing at a large picture of Lenin on the wall, he wondered why he had been summoned. The group of which he was a part had been invited to Moscow by the Russian Ministry of Education for the express purpose of grounding hundreds of Russian school teachers in the basic moral, spiritual, and doctrinal tenets of the Christian faith. But the invitation to this college had come suddenly and unexpectedly.

After brief pleasantries over tea and Russian pastries, Nash began to inquire why he was there. What did the Russian college, its president, and its faculty want from him? The president explained that his college was charged with preparing textbooks for all of Russia's public schools. Now that certain republics of the Soviet Union, including Russia, were abandoning the official hostility to religion that had characterized Soviet communism until recently, someone had decided to add information about the Christian faith to Russian textbooks. What assistance could Nash give, the president wondered, to the people who would write the new texts, specifically with regard to the Christian faith?

By the time this book appears, we hope, it will be obvious that the people of Russia, the Ukraine, the Baltic states, and other parts of the old Soviet empire are pursuing objectives that are really elements of a new liberation theology. They certainly want what later chapters of this book call political and economic liberation: democratic capitalism. But many influential reformers in these parts of the old Soviet Union know that if their dreams for their homeland are to be realized, moral and spiritual rejuvenation must also occur. As one of Boris Yeltsin's lieutenants put it in private conversation, "Seventy years ago, this country kicked God out. And ever since, there has been a moral and spiritual vacuum at the very center of this country, a vacuum that is largely responsible for the problems that have plagued us since the Revolution of 1917."

When the new leaders of the old Soviet Union or the new nations that the Soviet republics may become seek political, economic, and spiritual liberation, we have the major ingredients of a new and real liberation theology utterly unlike the so-called liberation theology pursued by Leftist thinkers in Latin America between 1965 and 1990. The new liberation theology repudiates almost all that the old liberationists stood for. This new liberation theology is the subject of this book.

The Worldview of the Old Liberation Theologians

The old liberation theology began sometime in the mid-1960s. The fundamental objective of the liberation thinkers, or so they said, was Christian action on behalf of the poor and the oppressed. As Gustavo Gutiérrez put it, "To believe is . . . to be united with the poor and exploited of this world from within the very heart of the social confrontations of 'popular' struggles for liberation."[1] Liberation theology urged eliminating oppression and poverty by replacing the economic and political structures alleged to cause them. If it proved necessary, the revolution might use violence. Liberation thinkers not only promoted and recommended revolutionary activity but also insisted that the Christian church should be at the very center of it. In Gutiérrez's words,

It is becoming more evident that the Latin American peoples will not emerge from their present status except by means of a profound transformation, a *social revolution*, which will qualitatively change the conditions in which they now live. The oppressed sectors within each country are becoming aware slowly, it is true, of their class interests and of the painful road which must be followed to accomplish the breakup of the status quo.[2]

1. Gustavo Gutiérrez, "Freedom and Salvation: A Political Problem," in Gustavo Gutiérrez and Richard Schaull, *Liberation and Change* (Atlanta: John Knox, 1977), 92.
2. Gustavo Gutiérrez, *A Theology of Liberation: History, Politics and Salvation*, trans. Caridad Inda and John Eagleson (Maryknoll, N.Y.: Orbis, 1973), p. 88.

Consequently, the old liberationists believed, the Christian church must become part of the revolutionary process, including its violence. According to Gutiérrez, "The Church's *mission* is defined practically and theoretically, pastorally and theologically, in relation to this revolutionary process."[3]

The Search for a Definition

According to George Weigel, president of the Ethics and Public Policy Center in Washington, D.C., liberation theology claims "that it is meet and proper for the Roman Catholic church to combat the 'sin' of suffering in poor nations by encouraging the establishment of socialist regimes, even through revolution."[4] Weigel, a Roman Catholic, can be excused for focusing on his own church despite liberation theology's many adherents among Latin American Protestants. Protestants played a role in the origin and early development of liberation theology in Latin America, and Protestant denominations and institutions in North America are active in spreading the liberation gospel.

Philip Berryman, an ex-priest turned liberation polemicist, insists that any adequate understanding of liberation theology also must acknowledge three other elements. First is an "interpretation of the Christian faith out of the suffering, struggle, and hope of the poor." As we will see, this interpretation, at least in Berryman's account, shows almost no respect for the content of the historic Christian faith. Second is a "critique of society and the ideologies sustaining it." But Berryman shows little interest in criticizing Left-wing ideologies. Third is "a critique of the activity of the church and of Christians from the angle of the poor."[5] Regrettably, however, Berryman equates "the angle of the poor" with the perspective he shares with other ideologists of the Left.

3. Ibid., 138, italics original.
4. George Weigel, "A New Opiate: Liberation Theology," *Insight*, March 2, 1987, 68.
5. Philip Berryman, *Liberation Theology* (Philadelphia: Temple University Press, 1987), 6.

Perhaps, then, we do best to forget Berryman's qualifications and simply state that liberation theology is a movement among Latin American Catholics and Protestants that has sought radical changes in the political and economic institutions of that region along what appear to be socialist or even Marxist lines. As Weigel explains,

> Liberation theologians have tended . . . to teach that class struggle is the basic dynamic of social life. They have taught that Latin America has been made, and is kept, deliberately impoverished and dependent by the rapacious capitalist North. They have argued for a partisan Church, identified with the underclass in the class struggle. They have taught that revolutionary violence is of less moral concern than the "first violence" of "sinful social structures." And they have claimed that politics takes priority over doctrine in identifying the truth or falseness of religious teaching.[6]

Liberation theology has appeared in several different packages. Sometimes it shows up in regional packages, making it necessary to distinguish Latin American from African and Asian varieties. It has also appeared in gender packages, leading one theologically liberal North American seminary to boast that it offers degrees in feminist liberation theology. One can also find ethnic packages that have produced black and Hispanic versions of liberation theology. This book focuses on the term's original sense, Latin American liberation theology. However, the problems and changes we will discuss in the original version of liberationism ought, under reasonable conditions, to carry over to its regional and ethnic varieties. Unfortunately, advocates of radical feminism do not seem especially open to influence from either empirical evidence or rational argument.[7]

6. Weigel, "A New Opiate: Liberation Theology," 68.
7. Radical feminists totally reject the laws of logical inference as part of an ideology that they associate with white European male oppression. It is not only difficult to reason with people who reject the laws of rational inference; it is impossible. For an elaboration of this point, see Ronald H. Nash, *Great Divides* (Colorado Springs, Colo.: NavPress, 1992).

Relatively moderate individuals, on the one hand, who use the liberation label and vocabulary but oppose violence and Marxist extremism must be distinguished from *radical liberation thinkers*, on the other hand, who appear captive to a Marxist ideology that often includes support for revolutionary violence. Richard John Neuhaus refers to the radicals as "hard utopians," by which he means hard-core Marxists.[8] In contrast, less radical liberationists seem content with exercises in consciousness-raising in connection with whatever cause possesses them at the moment. The utopianism of the more radical liberationists explains their immunity to such important evidence as the failure of socialism and the implications of the revolutions of 1989. In Neuhaus's words,

Utopian visions are immune to the manifest disasters of all Marxist-Leninist, social democratic, and democratic socialist experiments to date. Through the ruins of disappointed hopes, through rivers of blood and across the killing fields of utopias run amok, the Soviet Union, Cuba, China, Vietnam, Cambodia, and, very likely, Nicaragua, political pilgrims press on toward the great experiment that has still to be tried. One is not easily diverted from the question when at stake is nothing less than the Kingdom of God.[9]

The radical liberationists insist that the church should be at the center of revolutionary activity. It must become, they think, a part of the revolutionary process. This is often stated in a conveniently ambiguous way so that one can never be quite sure to what extent the revolutionary process is supposed to include violence.

Liberation theology teaches that the radical political transformation of the present order is a central component of living out the Christian faith. Revolutionary political action becomes, in theologies of liberation, the way to make Christian love for

8. See Richard John Neuhaus, *The Catholic Moment* (San Francisco: Harper and Row, 1987), 171.
9. Ibid., 172.

the poor truly effective. Failure to engage in the revolutionary struggle is failure to respond to the poor's yearning for liberation; it makes Christians oppressors. Since Jesus dwells in the poor in a hidden but real way, Christians not committed to the revolution have turned their backs on Christ. Commitment to "the revolution," then, is essential to what it means to be a Christian, or so say the liberation theologians.

Christian opponents of liberation thought have never disputed the Christian's obligation to care for the poor and to seek means to alleviate poverty and oppression. But they have always disputed the *agenda* by which liberationists insisted on fulfilling this duty. Among the most extreme representatives of the old liberationism, the so-called revolutionary Christians of Nicaragua under the Sandinistas, support for the Sandinista revolution was not simply permissible, it was a duty. For them, it was impossible to be a Christian in Nicaragua without supporting the Sandinistas' revolution.

Some Representatives of Liberation Theology

Gustavo Gutiérrez remains the dominant figure in Latin American liberation theology. Born in Peru in 1928, Gutiérrez was ordained a priest in 1959 after studying at several universities in Europe. His *Theology of Liberation* was published in Spanish in 1971; an English translation appeared in 1973. Gutiérrez has taught at several American universities, including Temple University and the University of Michigan. More recently, he has been a professor of theology at the Catholic University in Lima, Peru.

Rubem Alves was a Brazilian Protestant who published the first book to explain liberation beliefs: *A Theology of Human Hope* (1969).[10] Alves started out as an evangelical but lost his convictions after studying at the Presbyterian Seminary in Brazil. He presently regards himself as neither a liberation theologian nor, indeed, even a Christian. His career is a tragic exam-

---

10. Rubem Alves, *A Theology of Human Hope* (Washington, D.C.: Corpus, 1969).

ple of the harm that resulted from early efforts to radicalize idealistic young Latin Christians.

Hugo Assmann was born in Brazil in 1933. Until recently, he has been perhaps the most outspoken of liberation theologians, venting his hostility to capitalism in intemperate language. Assmann studied at several schools in Latin America and Rome. He has taught at Roman Catholic schools throughout Latin America and has been expelled from Brazil, Uruguay, Bolivia, and Chile for his radical views. His *Theology for a Nomad Church* (1976)[11] was one of the first books to explain and defend liberation themes. Recently, however, he has drawn attention for his willingness to explore capitalism as a means to alleviate poverty in Latin America.[12]

Juan Luis Segundo was born in Uruguay in 1925. After finishing studies in philosophy in Argentina, he like many other liberationists completed his education in Europe. His major impact on liberation theology came through more than fifteen books, including a five-volume work, *Theology for Artisans of a New Humanity*,[13] published in 1973–1974, and *The Liberation of Theology* (1976).[14] Segundo has been especially concerned with the pastoral implications of liberation theology.

José Porfirio Miranda, a Mexican, has published books with titles like *Marx and the Bible*[15] and *Communism in the Bible*.[16] Taking positions too fanciful even for many other liberationists, Miranda used to argue that, if they could only understand him correctly, Christians would see that Karl Marx was actually a better Christian than most professing believers. He reportedly

11. Hugo Assmann, *A Theology for a Nomad Church*, trans. Paul Burns (Maryknoll, N.Y.: Orbis, 1976).

12. See Hugo Assmann, "Democracy and the Debt Crisis," *This World* (Spring–Summer 1986): 83–103.

13. Juan Luis Segundo, *Theology for Artisans of a New Humanity*, 5 vols. (Maryknoll, N.Y.: Orbis, 1973–74).

14. Juan Luis Segundo, *The Liberation of Theology*, trans. John Drury (Maryknoll, N.Y.: Orbis, 1976).

15. José Porfirio Miranda, *Marx and the Bible: A Critique of the Philosophy of Oppression*, trans. John Eagleson (Maryknoll, N.Y.: Orbis, 1974).

16. José Porfirio Miranda, *Communism in the Bible* (Maryknoll, N.Y.: Orbis, 1982).

has abandoned many of his earlier views, which may explain why we have heard nothing from him recently.

Leonardo Boff, a Franciscan priest born in Brazil in 1938, has been in continual hot water with the Vatican for his allegedly heretical views. He has never hesitated to reinterpret or reject essential Christian beliefs in the service of his radical political ideology. Like many other early liberationists, Boff studied extensively in Europe. Two of his better-known books are *Jesus Christ Liberator* (1978) and *Liberating Grace* (1979).[17] His brother, Clodovis Boff, also born in Brazil (in 1944), is a priest and professor of theology at the Catholic University of São Paulo, Brazil. He works closely with base communities in Brazil. The brothers co-authored the book *Salvation and Liberation* (1984).[18]

Jon Sobrino, a Spanish Jesuit priest, teaches at the Jesuit University in El Salvador. His 1978 book, *Christology at the Crossroads: A Latin American Approach*,[19] reveals that even Christianity's historic teaching about Jesus Christ is not safe from liberationist attempts to redefine the faith. He has also co-authored *Theology of Christian Solidarity*,[20] a use of the word *solidarity* that would win no converts among the faithful believers who overthrew communism in Poland.

José Míguez-Bonino was born in Argentina in 1924. After studying at the Evangelical Theologate in Buenos Aires, Argentina, and at Emory University and Union Theological Seminary in the United States, Míguez-Bonino became the best-known Protestant liberationist in Latin America. He is an ordained Methodist clergyman with important ties to the World Council of Churches, an organization that has provided considerable

17. Leonardo Boff, *Jesus Christ Liberator: A Critical Christology for Our Time*, trans. Patrick Hughes (Maryknoll, N.Y.: Orbis, 1978) and *Liberating Grace*, trans. John Drury (Maryknoll, N.Y.: Orbis, 1979).

18. Clodovis Boff and Leonardo Boff, *Salvation and Liberation: In Search of a Balance between Faith and Politics*, trans. Robert R. Barr (Maryknoll, N.Y.: Orbis, 1984).

19. Jon Sobrino, *Christology at the Crossroads: A Latin American Approach*, trans. John Drury (Maryknoll, N.Y.: Orbis, 1978).

20. Jon Sobrino and Juan Hernández Pico, *Theology of Christian Solidarity*, trans. Philip Berryman (Maryknoll, N.Y.: Orbis, 1985).

assistance to Marxist-Christian efforts. He presently teaches theology at the Evangelical Institute of Advanced Theological Studies in Buenos Aires. His books include *Doing Theology in a Revolutionary Situation*[21] and *Christians and Marxists.*[22]

Enrique Dussel was born in Argentina in 1934. After studies in Argentina, he received doctorates from the University of Madrid and the Sorbonne in Paris. Exiled from his native Argentina for his radical views, Dussel presently teaches at the University of Mexico City. His books include *Ethics and the Theology of Liberation* (1978) and *History and the Theology of Liberation* (1976).[23]

As extreme as views described in the last few pages may sound, they were dominant among liberation theologians and their disciples during the 1970s and most of the 1980s. It is now possible, however, to detect cracks in the liberation fortress.

Signs of Change?

Several observers of liberation theology have detected signs of change in the movement. Princeton professor Paul Sigmund now distinguishes two phases. The earlier phase was admittedly Marxist, while the later one stresses the importance of base communities.[24] Arthur McGovern, a University of Detroit philosopher and Jesuit priest, explains, "The world of liberation theology is significantly different today than it was in the 1970s."[25]

According to Sigmund, almost all liberation theologians have changed in response to scholars' criticisms and changes in

21. José Míguez-Bonino, *Doing Theology in a Revolutionary Situation* (Philadelphia: Fortress, 1975).

22. José Míguez-Bonino, *Christians and Marxists* (Grand Rapids: Eerdmans, 1976).

23. Enrique Dussel, *Ethics and the Theology of Liberation*, trans. John Drury (Maryknoll, N.Y.: Orbis, 1978) and *History and the Theology of Liberation* (Maryknoll, N.Y.: Orbis, 1976).

24. See Paul Sigmund, "Whither Liberation Theology? A Historical Evaluation," *Crisis* (January 1987): 5.

25. Arthur F. McGovern, *Liberation Theology and Its Critics: Towards an Assessment* (Maryknoll, N.Y.: Orbis, 1989), 132.

Latin America and the Marxist world. For one thing, many have adopted more positive attitudes toward democracy. "They have also left behind much of the Marxist baggage with which the movement was encumbered in the early 1970s," he observes. While this hardly makes liberationists look favorably on capitalism, at least "they are willing to make use of the mechanisms of political democracy to moderate and restrain its excesses."[26] So, Sigmund concludes,

> Liberation theology does seem to have reached a new stage. It has abandoned most of the revolutionary rhetoric of the earlier period, concentrating on biblical and participatory themes, and appealing to what is now a mainstream element in official social teaching of the church, the preferential love for the poor. Even in the area of ecclesiology, the liberation theologians continue to insist on the importance of remaining in communion with the [Catholic] church hierarchy, although they criticize its pretensions to total control.[27]

Neuhaus agrees that liberation theology has entered a second stage:

> This second phase is said to be, among other things, more Christianly orthodox and much less Marxist than the liberation theology of the first phase. The evidence of such a major shift is still very sparse, but much has happened since the late sixties and early seventies and it would be surprising if these changes were not reflected in liberation theology in the years ahead. For example, it is generally acknowledged that the base communities have frequently resulted not in the revolutionary radicalization of the poor but in self-help movements of upward mobility toward middle-class achievement and traditional religious and moral allegiance. Further, the last decade in Latin America has witnessed a widespread movement toward democratization,

26. Paul Sigmund, *Liberation Theology at the Crossroads* (New York: Oxford University Press, 1989), 175.
27. Ibid.

and that has resulted in understandable changes in views of oppression and the revolutionary imperative.[28]

But Neuhaus adds an important qualification:

Talk about a second phase, however, should not divert attention from the fact that it is the first phase that is widely disseminated through Roman Catholic and Protestant seminaries and activist networks in North America today. . . . So even if what is now failed liberation theology will in the future be replaced by something else called liberation theology, the present state of the controversy will serve as a benchmark in Roman Catholicism's effort to give new definition to the paradox of the Church in the postmodern world.[29]

In other words, changes in liberation theology provide no excuse for ignoring what liberation theology once was and, in fact, still is among its more fanatical adherents, including many ecclesiastical leaders in North America.

Liberation theology *is* in transition. Some former extremists no longer wish to be considered liberation theologians at all. Others have begun to doubt that socialism is the solution they once thought it was. Some have begun to argue that Christian concern for the poor requires more careful thinking about economics, including a reevaluation of the role of capitalism, properly defined, in creating the wealth necessary if the poor are to receive lasting help. A few are toning down their Marxist rhetoric or even denying that they were really Marxists.

It is also possible to see signs of a more responsible handling of Scripture and a reappearance of traditional Christian themes, including, for example, an emphasis on spiritual matters. To the extent that such changes are sincere and not simply a reflection of a desire to avoid, say, the censure of the Vatican, they strengthen the hope that liberation theologians will remember that their first allegiance is to Jesus Christ and his

28. Neuhaus, *The Catholic Moment,* 177.
29. Ibid., 177–78.

gospel, not to the sociological, political, and economic dogmas of a Left-wing or Right-wing ideology.

The Revolutions of 1989

We can be grateful that some liberationists are toning down their rhetoric, their revolutionary ardor, their uncritical support for Marxism, and even their socialism. But it is important to see why these changes have occurred.

Some are, no doubt, a response to a decade or more of powerful criticisms, many of which we will examine in later chapters. Some result from changes in Latin America. But for any liberationist who was paying attention, events in formerly Marxist nations must have had some effect. Michael Novak has spoken to this point in his powerful article "Liberation Theology: What's Left."

Novak first suggests that the anti-socialist revolution that began in communist China, Eastern Europe, and the Soviet Union in 1989 has had a significant impact on liberation theology in Latin America. But he is disappointed that many have ignored or overlooked this issue thus far. One liberation theologian, whom Novak does not identify, has actually expressed the fear that East and West, once so estranged, will forget the South now that they are being reconciled. The irony of such a claim strikes Novak. Not too long ago, liberation theologians said they most feared "dependency" on the North. Now they seem to fear independence from the North.

Liberation theology depended heavily on the kind of Marxist thinking repudiated in Tiananmen Square and, more recently, in Red Square. The old myth that the world was divided into First World, Second World, and Third World no longer can be maintained, Novak argues. "The Second World" was never more than "a heavily armed version of the third world."[30] Novak cites Gorbachev's warning that by the start of the twenty-first century, the Soviet Union may have become a

---

30. Michael Novak, "Liberation Theology: What's Left," *First Things* (June/July 1991): 10. Novak's essay appears on pages 10–12 of the issue.

Third-World country on a par with nations like India. Equally damaging to the reputation and morale of liberation theologians are the Sandinistas' crimes and the evils of Cuba's police state.

In the post-1989 world, liberation theologians find themselves with two problems, Novak says, one economic and the other political:

> For two decades, liberation theologians blamed Latin American misery on "capitalist methods" such as markets, private property, and profits, and they looked for economic salvation by way of a "socialist" strategy of "basic needs." Often they had said of Eastern European socialist nations (as of Cuba) that, unattractive as they were in some respects, "at least they fulfill the basic needs of the people." But in 1989 Eastern Europeans spoke contemptuously of "basic needs" as a strategy fit for prisoners in jail, not for free human beings. And they clamored for capitalist methods as a source of liberation from *socialist* oppression.[31]

So what can liberation theologians who have spent two decades preoccupied with socialist methods that the socialist world itself now has abandoned possibly offer to the poor of Latin America? For example, Novak asks, what solution can they offer the poor to the massive problem of unemployment? By the start of the next millennium, fewer Latins will be employed in agriculture. But there also may be fewer jobs in enterprises run by transnational corporations because Leftist rhetoric has persuaded many such corporations to disinvest in the South. Where will the millions of new workers and unemployed older workers find jobs? His answer: they will need millions of new small businesses to provide not only the employment but also the goods and services needed by Latins, especially the poor. Such small businesses are the major engine of job-creation in modern economies. "It is sad to report," Novak continues, "that on matters relating to voluntary economic activity, business methods, laws of incorporation, mar-

31. Ibid.

ket pricing, enterprise, and the moral virtues required for economic development liberation theologians have had very little to say. Indeed, most of them remain to this day anti-capitalist by reflex."[32]

The collapse of socialism where it once held the status of a cult religion has exposed the major flaw of liberation theology. Former captives of that economic system so idolized by liberationists are, like the boy in Hans Christian Andersen's story, shouting out for all to hear, "The emperor has no clothes!" Are the liberationists really going to continue to claim that he is brilliantly attired? "As an economic idea," Novak writes, "socialism is now widely regarded as a mistake based on bad nineteenth-century economics. As a political idea, socialism is now widely regarded as too centralized and monolithic to secure basic human liberties. This leaves liberation theology's social theory in embarrassingly threadbare condition. . . ."[33] Any enterprise based on a social theory that is so demonstrably wrong is in serious trouble.

Novak suggests that the embarrassment conscientious liberationists must feel over all their misguided rhetoric and bad advice may be one reason why some have begun to give theology and spirituality higher priority. Some of the less honest liberationists are trying to rewrite history, suggesting that spirituality always was their primary concern. Novak is not persuaded. To be sure, he notes, spirituality can be found in earlier liberation writings; but it was hardly a central theme. In earlier times, he points out, liberationists "insisted on the inseparability of spirituality and revolutionary practice. They emphasized the concrete, material poverty of the poor and asserted that this poverty had to be overcome now, in this world, through dramatic social reconstruction. Indeed, they went so far as to accuse 'European' theology of inauthenticity because it was too abstract, too speculative, too removed from the daily life of the poor."[34] The older liberation theology was interested primarily

32. Ibid.
33. Ibid., 11.
34. Ibid.

in *praxis*, revolutionary action on behalf of the poor. Its theory was, Novak explains, "that through the practical work of building socialist societies, the poor of the third world would throw off the oppression they suffered at the hands of the first world, especially the United States."[35] Older liberationists' use of the Marxist Sandinistas and the Leninist Castro as models of what they hoped to accomplish makes today's talk about spirituality as the real essence of liberationism appear a calculated falsehood.

After these observations, Novak drives to his devastating conclusion. "It may be," he suggests, "that, chagrined over recent developments, liberation theologians have indeed moved from radical social reconstruction to Christian spirituality. If so, that is a development to be warmly welcomed. But in that case, one wonders what if anything remains of the original substance of the movement known as liberation theology."[36] So,

> if the liberationist "analysis" of poverty and oppression in Latin America can no longer be credited, what political hope for the future has been bequeathed to the poor by liberation theology? By all reports, pessimism and near-despair grip liberationists today, who see on the horizon very little indeed that offers hope of a better life to the poor of Latin America. But this darkness results from their own foreshortened vision. They have averted their eyes from, indeed, they have despised the type of political economy that has elsewhere lifted the poor out of poverty and given them institutions of liberty under which to prepare their children for a better life. The willful blindness of the liberation theologians, their unwillingness to search in the world of social theory beyond the lucubrations of socialism, has had very high costs for the poor during these past twenty years. . . . The collapse of the Marxist paradigm offers reason to hope that the costs of this misbegotten form of social analysis will not continue to be borne by the poor.[37]

35. Ibid.
36. Ibid., 12.
37. Ibid.

Novak's powerful indictment carries the suggestion that along with their newfound interest in spirituality, the older liberation theologians should be busy repenting for the harm their bad social theory and economics have done to the poor of the South.

In this introduction, we have offered an initial examination of liberation ideas and introduced some of the more important representatives of early liberation thought. We have also sought to show how out of step these ideas are with the world of the 1990s, in which most nations that modelled the socialism liberationists desired to impose on the people of Latin America now reject it.

It must be embarrassing to have placed all of one's liberation eggs in Marxism's basket. Realistically, how can people like this pretend to have any credibility? How can any Latin Americans who are aware of the Eastern European revolutions of 1989 and the Soviet revolution of 1991 respect self-proclaimed prophets of ideas these revolutions repudiated? With its present in such bad shape and its future in such doubt, liberation theology must change or die. In the following chapter, we will examine the history of liberation theology to see how it got to its present state of disarray.

Historical Overview

Anyone who desires to understand liberation theology adequately must grasp the major steps in its historical development. While we have tried to make this overview as simple as possible, we have attempted not to neglect any important event or development. Mention of a topic or individual in this brief historical survey does not preclude further comment later in the book.

Background Events in the 1950s and 1960s

Developments in Europe during the 1950s and 1960s. Latin American liberationists have insisted throughout the history of their movement that their theories were indigenous to Latin America. They claim that Latin thinkers developed these ideas to aid poor people in the South. Such claims contradict the evidence.

During the 1950s, many Latin clerics or future priests who became liberation theologians studied in Europe, where they absorbed many of the ideas that eventually became part of liberation thought. Some of these ideas appeared in Ernst Bloch's

1959 book, *Principle of Hope*, which drew parallels between Marxism and Christianity and suggested that the two need not be antithetic.

Some critics have claimed, as Richard John Neuhaus puts it, that "the North American understanding of [liberation theology] is based on bad English translations of bad Spanish translations of bad German ideas."[1] Neuhaus goes on to say that, whether that specific claim is true or not, "it is difficult to defend the claim that liberation theology is in any way indigenous to Latin America. The intellectual genealogy is almost entirely European, beginning with Karl Marx and running through Ernst Bloch, Jürgen Moltmann, Paulo Freire, and Johannes Metz. There is hardly a prominent concept in liberation theology that cannot be directly traced to a European source."[2]

While this observation hardly entails complete lack of originality in Latin liberation writings, it does remind us that liberation thought, at least in its early expressions, had a decidedly European air.

The establishment of Catholic "Centers for Social Investigation." After returning to Latin America, many of the aforementioned priests, radicalized by their European studies, became involved in founding Catholic "Centers for Social Investigation," where other Catholic intellectuals and clerics who had not studied in Europe were exposed to the radical ideas that were soon to dominate liberation thought.

The Cuban revolution (1959). The revolution that finally won Fidel Castro's forces control of Cuba in 1959 also played a role in shaping liberation thought in the decades that followed.

---

1. Richard John Neuhaus, *The Catholic Moment* (San Francisco: Harper and Row, 1987), 177. For examples of the sorts of things Neuhaus had in mind, see Johann B. Metz, *Faith in History and Society: Toward a Practical Fundamental Theology* (New York: Crossroad, 1979); Jürgen Moltmann, *The Theology of Hope* (New York: Harper and Row, 1967); and Dorothee Sölle, *Political Theology* (New York: Fortress, 1974).

2. Neuhaus, *The Catholic Moment*, 177.

Many Latins believed Castro's apparent success showed both the desirability and the possibility of similar Marxist revolutions in other Latin nations.

Castro's revolution gave Latin radicals a model of how other Latin American nations could deal with their social problems or so they thought. Of course, many liberationists' view of Castro as a cult hero was ironic for several reasons. He treated the church as an enemy and dealt harshly with many believers. Although liberationists continually denounced any sign of supposed Latin dependency on the United States, they kept silent about Cuba's almost total dependency on the Soviet Union. They refused to criticize Castro's totalitarianism, his persecution of Christians, his destruction of the Cuban economy, and his eagerness to pay for Soviet rubles and oil with the lives of Cuban soldiers fighting as Soviet proxies in places like Angola.

The establishment of the Conference of Latin American Bishops (CELAM). The Conference of Latin American Bishops began in 1955. Its first meeting was its only official gathering until CELAM II, which occurred in Medellin, Colombia, in 1968.

We do not suggest that the Conference of Latin American Bishops was an agent of liberationist policy. As we will see, the bishops disagreed strongly over issues raised by liberation thinkers. Nonetheless, the meetings of CELAM II in Medellin in 1968 and CELAM III in Puebla, Mexico, in 1979 provided important forums for the discussion and advancement of liberation ideas.

The debate over developmentalism and dependency. During the sixties, developmentalism became a popular theory for dealing with some problems in the Third World, especially in Latin America. Major elements in the growing radicalism of Leftist Catholics and Protestants were the repudiation of developmentalism and the rising influence of *dependency theory.*

According to dependency theory, the major reason for the persistent underdevelopment of the South is its dependency on

certain malevolent powers of the North. Spain first forced
Latin America into dependency. In the twentieth century, it is
said, the United States became the dominant source of Latin
dependency. The belief that nations like the U.S. were keeping
Latin America in continuing dependency fostered disillusionment among many intellectuals and students. True reform and
development were impossible, proponents of the theory
argued, lending support to the call for revolutions that would
emulate what had occurred in Cuba.

Uncritical acceptance of dependency theory strongly affected
other elements of liberation theory. Once accepted, the theory
blinded liberationists to any cause of Latin American poverty
that could not be traced to malevolent actions by the United
States and other nations of the North. Combined with the
belief that U.S. culpability for Latin poverty was a function of
so-called capitalism, it easily led to the conclusion that any adequate solution to poverty necessarily involves a fundamental
and revolutionary alteration of the structures of Latin American society and the repudiation of capitalism.

But there was another side to this coin. Wherever liberationists could be shown inadequacies in dependency theory, the
possibility arose that they might recognize other faults in their
system as well. Once they realized that they had misunderstood
the causes of poverty, they might also recognize that they had
misunderstood the solution.

Of course, the alleged developmentalism that became such
an object of hate was a sham. Developmentalism as conceived
in the sixties never had a chance to succeed because of continued interference by Latin America's ever-present statism.
Although liberationists labelled Latin America's prevailing economic systems capitalist, those systems actually were versions
of mercantilism, the very system Adam Smith hoped capitalism
would destroy. Later in this book we will try to eliminate the liberationist confusion over the nature of capitalism.

Early developments among Latin American Protestants. While
the rather primitive Marxism of early Roman Catholic libera-

tionism in Latin America came from Europe, liberationism
developed along a different track among Latin American Protestants. Among them, the major conduit of what became liberationist ideas was a small group of radicalized North American
missionaries and professors who carried their Leftist ideas to
Latin America.

For example, in 1962, Presbyterian missionary Richard
Schaull and liberal U.S. theologian Paul Lehmann toured Latin
American seminaries and Christian student groups, promoting
Left-wing ideas. While many outside of Latin America first
became aware of liberation theology following CELAM II, the
second meeting of the General Conference of Latin American
Bishops in Medellin, Colombia, in 1968, several Protestant
statements of liberationist views appeared prior to that meeting. The work of most of these Protestant writers grew out of
their contact with a movement known as ISAL (*Iglesia y
Sociedad en America Latin;* Church and Society in Latin America).

ISAL's formal organization in the early 1960s followed several years of Leftist agitation in the region by individuals and
agencies representing the World Council of Churches. At first,
the people associated with ISAL considered reform and development the best way to address Latin America's problems.
Gradually, however, those advocating reform either changed
their position or left ISAL. Revolution became ISAL's rallying
cry. ISAL blamed Latin America's problems on its dependency
on the North. With ISAL's evolving acceptance of the dependency thesis came its commitment to a full-blown socialist
agenda.[3]

Political ideology was not the only way in which the thinking
of people associated with ISAL was changing. Protestants who
turned to liberationism early in its history became increasingly
radicalized in their theology as well. For them, the starting
point for theology was no longer the authoritative Word of God;

3. For an account of all this by a Protestant liberationist, see José Míguez-Bonino,
*Doing Theology in a Revolutionary Situation: In Search of a Balance between Faith and Poli-
tics,* trans. Robert R. Barr (Philadelphia: Fortress, 1975), 54.

it was now what Marxists call "the historical situation." With their confidence in Scripture undermined by various forms of biblical criticism[4] and the authority of Scripture compromised by their newly-developed Marxist view of the importance of the historical situation, these ISAL Protestants came increasingly to view the Bible as irrelevant. About the only help they drew from Scripture was stories of ancient efforts to achieve liberation from poverty, suffering, and oppression.[5]

Thus, early Protestant liberationists who had been theologically orthodox or evangelical tended to abandon the high view of Scripture that was integral to their earlier evangelical faith. Eventually they rejected other essential elements of orthodox faith. Their "theology" often became little more than an elaborate rationale for the political ideology that ruled their lives.[6]

Like their Catholic counterparts, Protestant liberationists drew a great deal from non-Latin influences. Their peculiar reading of Karl Marx was influenced by Neo-Marxist philosophers like Herbert Marcuse. They were also influenced by German theologians like Moltmann and Dietrich Bonhoeffer.[7] Schaull, the American Presbyterian missionary mentioned earlier, became especially important in the development of Protestant liberationist thought in the South. As Emilio Nuñez explains:

4. For a critical analysis of these forms of biblical criticism, see Ronald H. Nash, *Christian Faith and Historical Understanding* (Richardson, Tex.: Probe, 1984).

5. Of course, the now radicalized Protestant liberationists maintained that even these stories were greatly embellished with myths and legends.

6. Emilio A. Nuñez documents this in his *Liberation Theology* (Chicago: Moody, 1985).

7. What became the official interpretation (which of course may not be the correct interpretation) of Bonhoeffer was as controversial as the liberationist understanding of Marx. For a detailed and critical account of the German roots of liberation thought, see Robert Walton, "Jürgen Moltmann's Theology of Hope," in *Liberation Theology*, ed. Ronald H. Nash (Grand Rapids: Baker, 1988). For a discussion of Marcuse's influence on liberationists in the South, see Nuñez, *Liberation Theology*, 76–77. For an evaluation of Marcuse's position, see Ronald H. Nash, *Social Justice and the Christian Church* (Lanham, Md.: University Press of America, 1992 [1st ed., 1983]), 97–102, and Ronald H. Nash, *Freedom, Justice and the State* (Lanham, Md.: University Press of America, 1980), 140–45.

Richard Schaull can be considered one of the pioneers of Latin American revolutionary theology. In his work *Encounter with Revolution*, published in 1955, Schaull arrives at the conclusion that in Latin America revolution is already a possibility and a necessity, that the Christian social doctrine of the past cannot adequately interpret the new situation of those countries, and that the Christian message has much to offer to properly guide the revolutionary process. Schaull's work shows the influence of neoorthodoxy and the theology of secularization.[8]

As a professor at the Presbyterian Seminary of Brazil, Schaull helped to radicalize some of his students; he also persuaded many Protestants associated with ISAL to believe that Christians are obligated to support revolutionary activity.

Rubem Alves entered the Presbyterian Seminary of Brazil as a committed evangelical preparing to work as an evangelist in Latin America. There his contacts with Schaull led him to abandon his evangelical faith and accept a radical political agenda. He produced the first systematic account of liberation theology. It included some tenets that soon became the unquestioned premises of liberation theology: (1) rich nations exploit poorer nations and keep them in a state of dependency; (2) the basic Latin American problem is a class struggle between rich (capitalists) and poor (proletariat); (3) both Christianity and Marxism aim at "humanization";[9] (4) God is revealed not in the Bible but in the events of history; (5) God is using Marxist revolutions to achieve his own ends; (6) Christians should join Marxists in fomenting Marxist revolutions. Alves also made it clear that his peculiar brand of Christian Marxism was not opposed to violence.[10]

For Alves, political power is an acceptable substitute for the Christian gospel. In his words, politics becomes "the new gospel, the annunciation of the good news that, if man emerges from

8. Nuñez, *Liberation Theology*, 64.

9. Alves ignored the obviously different ways in which Christianity and Marxism understand *humanization*.

10. For Alves's systematization of his views, see his *Theology of Human Hope* (Washington, D.C.: Corpus, 1969).

passivity and reflexivity, as the subject of history, a new future can be created. It challenges man: 'Seek first the kingdom of politics and his power, and all these things shall be yours.'"[11]

It is difficult to know what Alves believes in today. While he no longer regards himself as either a Christian or a liberation thinker, his 1969 book continues to influence generations of new readers.[12]

During the late 1960s, ISAL became increasingly isolated from the Protestant churches of the South. Given ISAL's rapid movement away from historic doctrinal and evangelistic concerns, this was hardly surprising. After its 1971 conference, ISAL expressed its intent to reestablish fellowship with the churches. Its purpose, however, was not to rejoin the historic Christian mission but to take its message of revolution into the churches and, by destabilizing and politicizing them, turn them into recruiting grounds for the liberationist cause.

ISAL ceased to exist as a formal organization in the early 1970s, but some Latin American thinkers like Nuñez believe it still represents "a solemn warning concerning the danger of allowing oneself to be obsessed by political problems and pretending to build a theological system not starting from the Scriptures, but from one's context and from social events, under the domination of an ideology."[13] Nuñez goes on to warn, "If the biblical norm for making theology is rejected, then there is no stopping on the slippery road that leads to a humanism that struggles to establish the kingdom of God here and now."[14]

Roman Catholic liberationism between Vatican II and CELAM II. The beginning point for this stage in the development of liberation theology was Pope John XXIII's call for the ecumenical council that became known as Vatican II. The sixties were a

11. Ibid., 16.

12. For illustrations of Alves's later positions, see *Tomorrow's Child: Imagination, Creativity, and the Rebirth of Culture* (New York: Harper and Row, 1972) and *What Is Religion?* (Maryknoll, N.Y.: Orbis, 1984).

13. Nuñez, *Liberation Theology*, 82.

14. Ibid.

time of ferment and revolution in Latin America as well as in the Roman Catholic Church. In his encyclical *Pacem in Terris* (1963), John XXIII called his church to become committed to democracy, human rights, and religious freedom. He urged it to update itself. However, few Catholics anticipated the full extent of "updating" that would come out of Vatican II.

The Council took place between October 1962 and December 1965, and John XXIII died before it ended. Left-wing Catholics interpreted its results in ways that encouraged movement toward radical political and theological beliefs. Perhaps Vatican II's major effect on liberation theology was that now appeals could be made to Council documents as pretexts for pursuing dialogue between Christians and Marxists. Since influential segments of Latin American Catholicism continued to oppose communism, especially in its Cuban incarnation, tensions continued to grow between conservative and radical elements of the Latin church.

The rise of guerrilla movements in the 1960s. During the 1960s, guerrilla movements born in nations like Venezuela, Guatemala, and Peru gave Latin Leftists two of their greatest heroes. During 1965, Camillo Torres, a radicalized priest, called on Christians to embrace revolution and ally themselves with Marxism. A year later, Torres died in a shootout between Marxist guerrillas and Colombian soldiers. In 1967, Castro's former lieutenant Ernesto ("Che") Guevara was captured and killed by Bolivian soldiers. As Paul Sigmund explains, both became patron saints "of the newly emerging Catholic Left, as well as [symbols] of the dangers of such Leftism to Catholic conservatives."[15] Disciples of liberation thought frequently displayed pictures of Jesus next to photos of Torres and Guevara.

The rise of Basic Christian Communities. The sixties also saw the rise of so-called Basic Christian Communities. In these

15. Paul Sigmund, *Liberation Theology at the Crossroads* (New York: Oxford University Press, 1989), 25.

small associations, usually in rural areas or on the fringes of cities, lay leaders minister to the community and guide them in
what is supposed to be a better understanding of the Bible,
God, themselves, and their relationship to their economic and
political environment. The communities use a process known
as *conscientization*, which is supposed to help them achieve a
greater consciousness of how to integrate their religious faith
with everyday social and political activities. Bible study is common in such communities. Unfortunately, the meaning of the
biblical text often is filtered through the Left-wing political ideology that has, until recently, been an indispensable part of the
communities' environment.

Although Sigmund cites estimates of the number of base
communities in Brazil alone as around 100,000 communities
serving 4 million people,[16] Michael Novak disputes such numbers as wildly inflated. Everyone, Novak notes, uses the same
numbers, and it is clear, he thinks, that no one is really count-
ing. If there is any growth in such communities, Novak contends, it is certainly much slower than the growth experienced
by evangelical Christian communities. Moreover, he points
out, "the concepts behind base communities in Latin America
antedate liberation theology and . . . the movement is in some
ways independent of it."[17] Whatever the truth on this matter,
one thing is apparent: one major way in which newer versions
of liberation theology differ from earlier forms is its movement
away from efforts to encourage revolutionary activity and
toward greater involvement with voluntary associations that
emphasize spiritual growth.

Liberationism from CELAM II Through CELAM III

The second meeting of the General Conference of Latin
American Bishops (CELAM II) took place in Medellin,
Colombia, in 1968. Outside Latin America, many first became

16. Ibid., 24–25.
17. Michael Novak, "Liberation Theology: What's Left," *First Things* (June/July
1991): 11.

aware of liberation theology because of the controversy that grew out of that conference.

Even though Gustavo Gutiérrez was outside the inner circle that controlled CELAM II, he attended the meeting and influenced the proceedings. His influence is apparent in several statements issued by the conference, like one claiming that "the principal guilt for the economic dependence of our countries rests with powers inspired by uncontrollable desire for gain." The statement added that "in many instances, Latin America finds itself faced with a situation of injustice that can be called institutionalized violence."[18] Unquestionably, following Medellin, liberation theology was news.

Events in Chile. Salvador Allende's rise to power in Chile in 1970 enhanced the influence of liberation theology. The event seemed to provide a model for the social transformation liberationists championed. Allende, a Marxist Socialist, was elected by a slim margin, carrying only 36 percent of the popular vote in a three-way race. The Chilean Communist Party, the largest in Latin America outside Cuba, was part of the coalition that helped him win. His control over Chile provided a sympathetic and supportive environment for the development of Leftist ideas. In 1971, an organization called Christians for Socialism met for the first time in Santiago. Its radical resolutions are discussed in a later chapter.

Late in 1971, Castro visited Chile and talked about "a strategic alliance" between Christians and Marxists. Speaking at the Chilean National Stadium, he emphasized "the necessity of uniting Marxist revolutionaries and Christian revolutionaries in an alliance based on the 'enormous points of coincidence' between the most pure precepts of Christianity and objectives

---

18. Excerpts from the Medellin documents may be found in Joseph Gremillion, *The Gospel of Peace and Justice* (Maryknoll, N.Y.: Orbis, 1976), 445–76. For the entire text of the documents, see *The Church in the Present-Day Transformation of Latin America in the Light of the Council*, vol. 2: *Conclusions* (Washington, D.C.: U.S. Catholic Conference, 1970). The quotation on this page appears in Paul Sigmund's article, "Whither Liberation Theology?" *Crisis* (January 1987), p. 7.

of Marxism."[19] Few people present noticed that he had forgotten to mention his own oppression and persecution of Christians in Cuba. On September 11, 1973, Allende's government was overthrown.

The Maryknoll Order and Orbis Books. Because of the location of its headquarters in Maryknoll, New York, the Catholic Foreign Mission Society of America is often referred to as the Maryknoll Order. As Neuhaus observes, the order was "established many years ago to win the world to Christ and his Church. Many remember Maryknollers chiefly for their heroic mission work in China."[20] But things changed dramatically. As liberal theology and the types of unbelief that always accompany it took over, the Maryknollers became practitioners of what is politely called religious pluralism. Neuhaus explains:

> Aficionados of irony will appreciate that years later (after their courageous and sacrificial work in helping take Christianity to China), during the rule of Chairman Mao, the Maryknollers would be promoting the view that China was the most Christian nation in the world, albeit without Christ and his Church. Carrying Karl Rahner's notion of "anonymous Christians" to an extreme, it is the triumph of the missionary enterprise by fiat. Certainly it is much more convenient than the heroic but apparently misguided course of Maryknollers of old who gave their lives to winning unbelievers for the Gospel one by one. So also in the supposed contest between atheism and Christianity, between totalitarianism and religious freedom, contemporary Maryknollers have again and again declared victory by redefinition.[21]

Like so many of the old liberationists, the Maryknollers lost their zeal for the gospel about the same time they began to champion liberationism. In 1970, the Maryknoll Order established Orbis Books, which quickly became the major publish-

19. Sigmund, "Whither Liberation Theology?" 7.
20. Neuhaus, *The Catholic Moment*, 172.
21. Ibid., 172–73.

ing outlet for liberation theology and theological liberalism in the Roman Catholic Church. In 1973, Orbis Books published the English translation of Gutiérrez's book *A Theology of Liberation*. The rest, as they say, is history.

Nicaragua and the Sandinistas. With the Sandinistas playing a prominent but by no means exclusive role, the people of Nicaragua overthrew the hated dictator Anastasio Somoza in July 1979. Quickly breaking their promises, the Sandinistas consolidated control and began marching Nicaragua down the road to Marxism.[22] Few Sandinista leaders were Christians in any biblical and traditional sense.

Under different circumstances, they might have treated the Nicaraguan church as Castro treated the church in Cuba. But the situation in Nicaragua differed enough to require other tactics. Peasants and workers with strong religious convictions often have been the strongest opponents of communism. This was certainly true in Poland and was likely to be true in Nicaragua, two of the most heavily Roman Catholic nations in the world. Liberation theology afforded hard-line Marxist-Leninists a way to defuse religious opposition to Marxism in Nicaragua. If Catholic peasants could be persuaded that Marxist values really were Christian values, their initial resistance could be weakened significantly. What made the Sandinistas' tactic even more promising was having their own radicalized priests or pastors teach the peasants the "Christian" version of Marx. After the peasants' initial opposition to Marxism wore down, efforts could be made to win the new Marxist "Christians" to the more radical views of Marxism-Leninism.

In other words, the Sandinistas used liberation theology as an anesthetic while they removed the patient's Christianity. Liberation theology could be the Trojan horse by which Marxism-Leninism gained access to nations that otherwise would

22. Humberto Belli tells the story of these events in *Breaking Faith: The Sandinista Revolution and Its Impact on Freedom and Faith in Nicaragua* (Westchester, Ill.: Crossway, 1985). We present evidence of the kind of solidarity the Marxist Sandinistas felt with Soviet Marxism-Leninism in chapter 3 of this book.

have rejected it on religious grounds. Even liberationist José Míguez-Bonino acknowledges the extent to which liberation theology can help overcome religious opposition to communism.[23]

The importance of Christianity to the Nicaraguan revolution did not involve a change in the Marxist philosophy of the Sandinistas or an openness or new tolerance toward religion. It simply meant a new consciousness of the need to *use* Christians and, as a corollary, a tactical decision not to present an openly antireligious face. Professed Nicaraguan Christians who supported the revolution encouraged other Christians to work with the Sandinista government. They did this by reinterpreting Christian beliefs to endorse the main Marxist-Leninist tenets regarding man and society. They claimed that true Christianity is, in fact, Marxism.[24]

Cooperation between Christians and Marxists in Nicaragua under Sandinista rule led many Christians to abandon their religious faith and convert to atheistic communism.[25] It is interesting that in his *Christians and Marxists* Míguez-Bonino showed no interest in inviting Marxists to become Christians. One searches in vain through his "dialogues" with Marxists for any declaration of the gospel.

Christian supporters of the Nicaraguan revolution lent credibility to the Sandinista contention that the Sandinistas were not Marxist-Leninists but a novel regime in which Christianity and revolution could walk together. In truth, these "revolutionary Christians" became a visible front to attack the Christian churches of Nicaragua and to undermine their authority and teachings, thus minimizing for the Sandinistas the potentially high cost of a more direct confrontation with the Catholic Church. Ironically, the revolutionary Christians also helped hide from the view of Christians abroad the fact that there was

23. See José Míguez-Bonino, *Christians and Marxists* (Grand Rapids: Eerdmans, 1976), 25, 26.

24. For more on this, see Humberto Belli, "Nicaragua: Field Test for Liberation Theology," *Pastoral Renewal* (September 1984): 30, 31.

25. For more specifics about all this, see Belli, *Breaking Faith*.

religious persecution in Nicaragua throughout the years of Sandinista rule.[26] While liberation theology in Nicaragua originally inspired Christians to oppose a Right-wing dictatorship, it later became a tool to justify support for a Left-wing dictatorship. In Nicaragua, at least, Marxist-Leninists found a Trojan horse that let them inside the gates of power.

But then the Sandinistas were defeated in the election of early 1990. It is difficult to find words to describe their actions during the two months between their electoral defeat and Violeta Chamorro's inauguration as Nicaragua's democratically elected president. *Time* magazine provided details under the headline "The Sandinistas' Greedy Goodbye."[27] Referring to their "shameless pillaging" of the country, *Time* reported that the Sandinistas looted the country of as much as $700 million worth of booty. According to *Time*, they stole $24 million from Nicaragua's Central Bank. Former president Daniel Ortega now lives in a confiscated house valued at $950,000. Miguel D'Escoto, a priest and foreign minister of Nicaragua under the Sandinista regime, now owns one of the more expensive mansions in Managua acquired for a mere $13,000. Others near the top of the Sandinista hierarchy profited as well.

Needless to say, the Sandinistas have given none of this $700 million of land, property, and cash to ease the poverty and misery of Nicaragua's poor. Not surprisingly, old liberationists and utopian Leftists who control so many centers of religious power in the United States have yet to criticize their greedy profiteering. Beyond Marxists' revolutionary rhetoric lies their true objective: accumulating power and wealth.

CELAM III. The third meeting of the General Conference of Latin American Bishops occurred at Puebla, Mexico, in January and February of 1979. Liberation theology was still largely an intellectual curiosity until Puebla. The controversy generated by CELAM III, especially a major address by Pope John

---

26. Once again, details are in Belli's *Breaking Faith*.
27. "The Sandinistas' Greedy Goodbye," *Time*, June 24, 1991, 34.

Paul II that clearly criticized many features of liberation theology, attracted attention around the world.

By the end of the 1970s, Roman Catholic bishops critical of Marxism including Alfonso Lopez Trujillo, now cardinal of Medellin, had gone on the offensive. Position papers distributed before the conference severely criticized liberation theology. Liberationists and their supporters realized that Puebla would be a major ideological battlefield. While no prominent liberation thinkers were invited as experts, sympathetic bishops extended invitations to some, including Gutiérrez, who conducted press conferences and meetings outside the official conference. The liberationists attacked the preliminary papers and agitated on behalf of their position.

In his address to the conference, John Paul II criticized efforts to politicize the gospel and to develop any so-called people's church. He argued for a "Christian concept of liberation that cannot be reduced simply to the restricted domain of economics, society and culture." He warned about people who

> depict Jesus as a political activist, as a fighter against Roman domination and the authorities, and even as someone involved in the class struggle. This conception of Christ as a political figure, a revolutionary, as the subversive from Nazareth, does not tally with the church's catechesis. . . . [But] Jesus . . . unequivocally rejects recourse to violence. He opens his message of conversion to all. . . . His mission . . . has to do with complete and integral salvation through a love that brings transformation, peace, pardon, and reconciliation.[28]

The final document of the conference was a compromise; neither side won. While it condemned Marxism and the politicization of theology, it also criticized liberal capitalism. But careful students of capitalism quickly pointed out that the "liberal capitalism" attacked at Puebla was a straw man.

28. John Paul II, "Opening Address at Puebla," in *The Pope and Revolution: John Paul II Confronts Liberation Theology*, ed. Quentin L. Quade (Washington, D.C.: Ethics and Public Policy Center, 1982), 53, 54.

Vatican Documents and Papal Encyclicals in the 1980s

Liberation theology in the eighties has come under pressure from several directions. Some came from a series of documents and encyclicals released by the Vatican.

"Instruction on Certain Aspects of Liberation Theology" (1984). This document reflected the concerns of Cardinal Joseph Ratzinger over dangers liberation theology posed to Roman Catholicism. Ratzinger was troubled by liberation theology's connections with Marxism. No less dangerous, he thought, were its attempts to politicize the church and the new vision many liberationists had of the Catholic Church's organizational structure.

While the 1984 Instruction refused to name specific liberationists, Latin Americans could easily see allusions to Gutiérrez and other well-known liberation activists. The Instruction criticized these unnamed liberationists for uncritically accepting the allegedly scientific character of Marxist claims, for supporting violence, and for politicizing the church and its teachings.

The Instruction portrayed radical liberation theology as a perversion of the Christian message. While it acknowledged the existence of more moderate versions of liberation thought, it condemned radical varieties for borrowing uncritically from Marxist ideology, for affirming violence as part of the revolution, and for using liberal methodology in handling Scripture. Marxist ideology leads, the Instruction insisted, to totalitarianism. It ignores the spiritual nature of human beings; therefore it subordinates individual persons to the collective whole. It is incompatible with a belief in human dignity. Moreover, liberation theology leads to a dangerous elitism in which only those who agree with the liberationist's view of revolutionary praxis are thought to have the truth. It rejects moral standards outside the camp of the revolutionaries. Furthermore, it confuses the poor with Marx's proletariat. This turns the church of the poor into a vanguard of the revolution.

The gospel of the radicals is a purely earthly gospel, nothing more than the pursuit of earthly objectives. Liberationist hermeneutics leads to a political rereading of the Bible, reducing the meaning of Scripture to an exclusively political message. Moreover, more radical versions of liberation thought lead to a liberal view of the Bible, as well as of Jesus and his mission. They see Jesus' death in purely political terms and hence deny both its salvific value and God's plan of redemption.

The 1984 Instruction was an uncompromising critique of radical, utopian versions of liberation thought. It criticized ministers who separate the sharing of bread from the sharing of the Word of God. It attacked those who minimized evangelism and reduced the gospel to a purely earthly political and economic message. It warned against the uncritical use of Marxist concepts that leads to positions inconsistent with historic Christianity. And it criticized liberationists for their blindness to the totalitarian Left's enslavement of people.

"Instruction on Christian Freedom and Liberation" (1986). The 1984 Instruction promised a second statement. That appeared eighteen months later, in April of 1986. By any account, it was more moderate than its predecessor. It actually endorsed a variation of one of liberationism's favorite phrases: "preferential *love* for the poor." It countenanced Basic Christian Communities so long as they did not divide local churches and the universal church. It even sanctioned armed revolt as a last resort to end tyranny, although this hardly justified violent revolution, as many liberationists claimed.

Various supporters of liberationism attempted to interpret the 1986 Instruction as contradicting the 1984 Instruction, making it an implicit endorsement of liberation theology. Looking back, however, it is now apparent that the 1986 document was in fact an early step toward a dramatically new and totally different kind of liberation theology, the shape of which would become clearer in papal encyclicals of 1988 and, especially, 1991. The 1984 and 1986 Instructions are totally compatible. The earlier document had to make clear the Catholic Church's break with the radical and utopian versions of liberation thought before the later one could begin to explore what a new liberation theology would look like. As things turned out, it took another five years to complete this exploration.

Sollicitudo Rei Socialis (1988). John Paul II's encyclical *Sollicitudo Rei Socialis* was clearly the product of many hands, and the resulting lack of consistency is obvious.[29] The outcome is less than satisfactory, reminding many of a sermon in which the preacher tries to do too many things and ends up doing none well. Writing in *National Review*, British thinker John Gray wondered aloud if perchance the pope had become "The Last Socialist." Gray began by noticing how some on the Left viewed *Sollicitudo* as a conversion of the pope to the doctrine of "moral equivalence." This is the Leftist notion that there has been no significant moral difference between the United States and the Soviet Union. The Soviets have their sins and the Americans have theirs; there is little basis to choose morally between them.

While Gray criticizes much in *Sollicitudo*, he objects strenuously to attempts to read moral equivalence into the document. Such thinking, he contends, "neglects the complex and difficult circumstances in which [the pope] must address constituencies within the Church that have radically divergent histories and outlooks. The Pope must address both Catholic believers who (like those in Poland) have had ample experience of the material poverty and spiritual emptiness of Marxian socialism and the Catholics of Western Europe and North and South America who, lacking such experience, are captivated by the hallucinatory visions of liberation theology."[30] So much for the alleged endorsement of moral equivalence!

29. The full text of the document is reprinted in *Aspiring to Freedom: Commentaries on John Paul II's Encyclical 'Social Concerns'*, ed. Kenneth A. Myers (Grand Rapids: Eerdmans, 1988), 3–63. The text is accompanied by helpful essays by Richard John Neuhaus, Michael Novak, George Weigel, and others.

30. John Gray, "The Last Socialist?" *National Review*, June 30, 1989, 27. Gray's article appears on 27–31.

But other criticisms of the 1988 document are justified, in Gray's view. For one thing, he writes, the encyclical "endorses a baseless and misleading history of Western capitalism and of the West's relations with developing nations. It does not support Marxian notions of class struggle, but it propagates a socialist caricature of unfettered capitalism, and it envisions an alternative to both capitalism and socialism that is, in the end, only a mirage."[31] While some aspects of capitalism deserve criticism, Gray insists, it makes no sense for the Vatican to endorse radical alternatives to the economic system that has brought both liberty and prosperity to so much of the world. Gray goes on to note that

> all contemporary evidence suggests that it is the adoption of the institutions of the market economy that is the chief condition of sustained economic development. . . . the role of capitalist institutions in the developing world is that of a pacemaker for economic growth, while socialist institutions are a recipe for continued poverty (and often famine). . . . it is simply false to suppose that underdevelopment is caused by Western capital.[32]

None of this obliges defenders of capitalism to become blind to its faults.

> Democratic capitalism, like any other economic and political system, is heir to the evils that flow from man's intractable limitations and can be defended only as the least imperfect set of institutions available to mankind in the present age. . . . the Christian life best thrives in the economic system which the papal encyclicals have condemned. . . . radical alternatives to market capitalism are merely delusive, and the idea of a third way between capitalism and socialism is a distraction from the task of reforming our historical inheritance of capitalist institutions so that all may benefit from them.[33]

31. Ibid., 27.
32. Ibid., 31.
33. Ibid.

A major handicap in all such discussions is the almost universal confusion about the essential nature of capitalism. As later discussions in this book will make clear, capitalism often gets blamed for problems created by a different economic system called interventionism or the mixed economy. While proponents of interventionism love to claim that governmental interference with a market economy is necessary to prevent negative economic consequences or unjust results, the truth is altogether different. Intervention in the economy helps sinful people to concentrate economic power, thus producing results that are the precise opposite of those promised by interventionists. Statist interference with market processes is also counterproductive because it causes other unintended consequences like inflation and depressions.[34]

But Gray gives the pope high marks for repeatedly distancing "himself from the Manichean certainties of liberation theology by stressing, on his visits to Latin America, that, although the Church must concern itself with questions of the distribution of political power and economic resources, yet in a Christian perspective salvation comes as a spiritual transformation, not a social revolution."[35]

With the 1991 publication of *Centesimus Annus* (which we will discuss shortly), it is much easier to place *Sollicitudo* in proper perspective. Except for the faulty economics already noted, and the pope's need in the mid-eighties to appear even-handed in the ongoing struggle between East and West, it is now clear that the 1988 document was one more step in the evolution of a new liberation theology. Roberto Suro quotes Rocco Buttiglione, an Italian thinker close to the pope, as saying, "This encyclical [*Sollicitudo*] offers a new Liberation Theology. . . . It is a new Liberation Theology that surpasses the limits of the old one that is so thoroughly grounded in the Latin American experience and it is a theology that knows Communists."[36]

34. Such claims surprise many people. For more details on all this and references to the huge body of literature available, see Ronald H. Nash, *Poverty and Wealth: Why Socialism Has Failed* (Richardson, Tex.: Probe, 1992 [1st ed., 1986]).

35. Gray, "The Last Socialist?" 28.

36. Cited in Roberto Suro, "The Writing of an Encyclical," in *Aspiring to Freedom*, ed. Myers, 162–63.

This comment not only encourages us today to see *Sollici-tudo* as a step toward the much more mature and complete statement in the 1991 encyclical, but also helps us recognize more clearly some truly powerful comments in the 1988 document that were overlooked in all the confusion. As an example, consider the following:

> It should be noted that in today's world, among other rights, *the right of economic initiative* is often suppressed. Yet it is a right which is important not only for the individual but also for the common good. Experience shows us that the denial of this right, or its limitation in the name of an alleged "equality" of everyone in society, diminishes, or in practice absolutely destroys the spirit of initiative, that is to say *the creative subjec-tivity of the citizen*. As a consequence, there arises, not so much a true equality as a "leveling down." In the place of creative initiative there appears passivity, dependence and submission to the bureaucratic apparatus which, as the only "ordering" and "decision-making" body if not also the "owner" of the entire totality of goods and the means of production, puts everyone in a position of almost absolute dependence, which is similar to the traditional dependence of the worker-proletarian in capitalism.[37]

The obvious allusions to the captive peoples of Eastern Europe in this paragraph provide a helpful reminder that the world was a much different place in 1988 than in 1991. *Sollici-tudo* was written before anyone, including the pope, whose Pol-ish homeland was fighting for liberation against its communist rulers, could have dreamed what changes would be wrought by the revolutions of 1989. The paragraph also provides hints that someone in the Vatican had been reading the writings of Michael Novak.[38]

37. John Paul II, *Sollicitudo Rei Socialis*, in *Aspiring to Freedom*, 16.
38. Readers familiar with Michael Novak's work will have no difficulty recognizing the paragraph's use of ideas from *Will It Liberate? Questions about Liberation Theology* (Mahwah, N.J.: Paulist, 1986).

While *Sollicitudo* was being written, the Vatican faced a serious dilemma. On the one hand, it wanted to counter the efforts of radical liberation thinkers to dilute the Christian gospel with Marxist politics. On the other hand, it also wanted to increase its opportunities to preach the Christian message in Marxist countries. This second objective meant that it could not appear to be biased in favor of the West. *Sollicitudo* is the awkward consequence of the Vatican's attempt to walk this tightrope. A transitional work produced by many hands at a difficult and ambiguous time, it grew from a desire to advance the discussion of liberation, even move it to the higher plane we find gloriously displayed in the 1991 encyclical. As such, its significance pales in comparison with the pope's 1991 encyclical, *Centesimus Annus*.

Centesimus Annus (1991). John Paul II issued this encyclical in honor of the hundredth anniversary of *Rerum Novarum*, Pope Leo XIII's encyclical of 1891.[39] Neuhaus admits that "in retrospect, it can be seen that *Sollicitudo* was preparing the way for *Centesimus*, but it must frankly be acknowledged that almost nobody was prepared for the present encyclical's comprehensive affirmation of the market economy. The free market, according to the Pope's argument, is the economic correlate of a Christian understanding of human nature and responsibility."[40]

Left-wing Catholics, including a full complement of liberation theologians, have not quite known what to do with such an unabashed denunciation of socialism and what is quite simply the strongest Vatican endorsement of capitalism in history. Not surprisingly, many Leftists have tried to put their usual spin on the document, but the text simply will not support it. Any Leftists who hope to demonstrate from the text that the pope sup-

39. The full text of *Centesimus Annus* appears in *Origins*, May 16, 1991, CNS Documentary Series. A condensed version under the title "The Economics of Human Freedom" was published in *First Things* (August/September 1991): 36–45.

40. Richard John Neuhaus, "That Encyclical," *First Things* (August/September 1991): 11.

ports zero-sum theories of economic redistribution is welcome to try. As George Weigel points out, the document is so bold that it is "likely to redraw the boundaries of the Catholic debate over the right-ordering of culture, economics, and politics for the foreseeable future."[41] Weigel goes on to note that "the text of *Centesimus Annus* itself is plain: the authoritative teaching of the Catholic Church is that a properly regulated market, disciplined by politics, law, and culture, is best for poor people. It works. And it gives the poor an 'option' to exercise their freedom as economic actors that is available in no other system."[42]

The publication of *Centesimus Annus* finally makes clear what the Vatican has struggled to bring forth in the decade since the pope's address at Puebla. It is nothing less than the formulation of a new liberation theology, one that rejects totally the *means* of the old liberation theology but retains its *end* of offering the poor and oppressed peoples of the world true liberation in every sense of this vitally important word.

The dramatic changes in the world between the mid-1960s and late 1991 show that the old liberation theology is hopelessly outdated. Reflecting on how eagerly many old liberationists subordinated the eternally true message of the Christian gospel to social theories now widely discredited, it is difficult to avoid enormous sadness. As we have seen, however, others have been busy pointing in the direction of a new liberation theology that offers hope for genuine liberation from poverty and oppression without betraying the historic mission of the Christian church. These individuals, both Catholic and Protestant, have clearly moved beyond the old liberation theology.

41. George Weigel, "The New, New Things: Pope John Paul II on Human Freedom," *American Purpose* (May-June 1991): 33.
    42. Ibid., 38.

2

Toward a New Liberation Theology

*T*his chapter differs from others in the book. It not only summarizes what many regard as the most important Christian objections to liberation theology in the 1980s, but also packages them as a single polemic against the position. To its several singular objections it adds the cumulative point that the old liberation theology no longer deserves serious consideration. The day rightfully belongs to a new version of liberation thought. We do not intend to suggest that this chapter stands on its own. Rather, our purpose in placing this line of argument at this point in the book is twofold: to show readers what a relatively brief and blunt assault on liberationism during the 1980s looked like and, by doing so, to place a number of objections on the table. Following chapters will examine the support for these arguments in more detail.*

Many Christians have rejected liberation theology in its entirety because they disagreed with specific elements of it. Yet early versions of liberation theology had at least one thing right: committed Christians ought not to remain silent and inactive about the horrible plight of the world's poor. Concern for genuine liberation occupies an important place in Christian belief and practice.

Unfortunately, several errors in older versions of liberation theology blunted the effectiveness of liberationists' concern and action and made them advocates of policies guaranteed to forestall or even kill genuine liberation. On the way to their counterproductive policies, many liberationists also lost sight of the essential doctrinal component of the historic Christian faith. Bad economics was one thing; theological heresy was another.

Some people believe the first call for a *new* liberation theology appeared in a 1983 book, *Social Justice and the Christian Church*.[1] Similar concerns are obvious in many publications by Michael Novak, and some observers have suggested that the vision of a new liberation theology can be found in the major Vatican statements on the subject published during the 1980s.

Our title suggests three questions: (1) What was and still is the *old* liberation theology? (2) Why must the *old* liberation theology be replaced by a newer version? (3) What are some of the more important ways in which a *new* liberation theology constitutes an advance over the earlier versions?

The Old Liberation Theology

Christian theology often is portrayed as emphasizing thought over action; indeed, it is pictured as stressing thought about other-worldly matters over thought about problems in this world. The older liberation theologians claimed to represent a newfound Christian concern for the poor and oppressed peoples of the world. They followed Karl Marx's advice to stop thinking about the world and start changing it. They stressed the need for concrete action on behalf of poor and oppressed people.

Unfortunately, liberation thinkers tended to ignore the important differences between means and ends. They showed

1. See Ronald H. Nash, *Social Justice and the Christian Church* (Lanham, Md.: University Press of America, 1992 [1st ed., 1983]).

little tolerance for other Christians who shared their *goal* of aiding the poor but advocated different *means*. Older liberation theologians almost universally preferred policies and programs that they themselves identified as Marxist.

While some recent propagandists for the old liberation theology now try to cover up the movement's earlier Marxism, more than the rhetoric was Marxist. Their writings simply assumed that the major reason for the poverty and oppression of Latin America was American-style "capitalism" and the dependence of Third World nations on "capitalist" nations like the United States. Given their universal acceptance of this questionable claim, it was only natural for them to believe the remedy for poverty was a revolution that would dramatically alter the structural injustices, end the dependence of the South on the North, and replace what they called capitalism with what they called socialism.

Of course, anyone calling himself a liberation *theologian* would seem obliged to say something that sounds biblical and Christian. This side of the equation was covered by frequently bizarre readings of the Bible designed to show that, when read correctly, the Bible endorses a Marxist approach to economic redistribution. Each appearance of the word *justice* in the Bible is supposed to imply divine endorsement for *social justice,* a term the liberationists left undefined. Some even found ways to read Marx in a new way, turning him into a "Christian." (Using key words in vague, fuzzy ways often appears to be a precondition for being a liberation theologian.)

The old liberationists developed a new way of reading and interpreting the Bible. The Bible must be read, they said, from the perspective of the poor and oppressed (two categories they generally and often erroneously equated). That is, the concrete, historical situation of the poor must be the key to determining which passages of the Bible are most important or inspired and how they are to be understood. (Radical feminist theologians employ a similar hermeneutic, teaching that only those parts of the Bible that speak about the oppression of women are the Word of God. They therefore know, a priori, that segments of the Bible that ignore or contradict their beliefs are uninspired, untrue, and unimportant.) This neo-liberal approach to the Bible remains an important presupposition of the older liberation theologians. They bring their own criteria of authenticity and authority to their reading of the Bible. Whatever they find in Scripture that cannot be forced into their preconceived pattern they simply ignore or reject.

Uninformed Christians who fail to understand the liberationist hermeneutic often get excited when they find Third World Christians in liberationist "base communities" reading, even studying, the Bible. What they neglect is the cultic way these Christians are taught to twist the biblical message to fit the liberationist ideology.

A Critique of the Old Liberation Theology

Soon after liberation theology arose, some Christian critics began questioning liberationists' commitment to essential Christian beliefs, their economic competence, their commitment to democracy, and their opposition to violence and totalitarianism. Christian opponents of the old liberation theology heartily affirm the Christian's obligation to care for the poor and seek means to alleviate poverty and oppression. What they object to is the means or the agenda of earlier liberationists. Since the movement presents itself as a type of *theology*, we should test the soundness of its religious beliefs. Since it calls itself *liberation* theology, we should examine the extent to which it really does liberate, both economically and politically.

Indeed, Christians should test any alleged liberation theology by three criteria: (1) Will it really liberate people from poverty (economic liberation)? (2) Will it really free people from tyranny (political liberation)? (3) Will it really do what Christianity is supposed to do: deliver people from sin (spiritual liberation)?

There is nothing arbitrary about these three tests. Only a system that delivers on all three forms of liberation is a true liberation theology. Any system that fails to deliver on any one is a false liberation theology.

Economic liberation. Liberation theologians say a lot about poverty. One crucial claim is that putting their theology into practice liberates people from it.

Unfortunately, liberation theology cannot offer a proper remedy for poverty because it fails to understand the problem. The old liberation theology rested on the myth that poverty results exclusively from one person or nation exploiting another. Economic exchange, for liberationists, always means a zero-sum game in which if one person wins, another must lose. They have always found it inconceivable that voluntary (market) exchanges are a positive-sum game, one in which all participants can win.

What old liberationists did best was blame others for the problems of their region or nation. But First World capitalist nations are *not* responsible for Third World poverty, which is older than capitalism and, in fact, was once far worse than it is now. Colonialism, or dependence, is neither a necessary nor a sufficient condition for Third World poverty. Some of the most developed areas in the world today (Malaysia and Singapore, to cite two examples, not to mention the United States and Canada) were once colonies, while some of the poorest nations (Afghanistan and Ethiopia) never were.

Especially ironic is the persistent liberationist effort to blame capitalism for the poverty of Latin America. As Novak has shown, Latin America has never been capitalist. Its economic ills clearly flow from *too much* statist control, not too little. It is bizarre, then, to hear liberationists declaring that their "solution" to Latin America's economic woes is even more of the kinds of statist control that created and perpetuated its problems in the first place. More often than not, poverty in a nation is fostered by the stupidity or corruption (often both) of the heavy-handed leaders of the state. Socialism makes such stupidity and corruption more deadly by concentrating economic and political power in the hands of the politically and militarily powerful.

While everything possible must be done to encourage economic growth in the Third World, socialism is useless in such a task. As Novak has argued repeatedly, "Socialism was not invented as a system designed to produce economic development. Its main historical purpose has been political control."[2]

Wealth does not arise by accident or governmental fiat. It results rather from the kinds of human action and social cooperation that are so basic to that economic system called capitalism. When people pay proper attention to the necessary role that the creation of wealth must play in liberating people from poverty, they see clearly that capitalism offers the poor their only real hope of economic deliverance. Liberation thinkers never mention formerly poor nations like Taiwan, Singapore, and Hong Kong, which have achieved some of the highest rates of economic growth in the world. Perhaps they ignore them because they succeeded by consciously rejecting socialism and adopting capitalism.

Particularly enlightening is the history of Taiwan's economic development, told by Kwoh-ting Li, former Taiwanese minister of economic affairs and minister of finance, in *Economic Transformation of Taiwan (R.O.C.)*. Li sums up the government's strategy in "two principles": "One is the maintenance of private property and the market mechanism in an environment favouring private enterprise. . . . The other is the maintenance of an equitable distribution of income as society becomes more affluent and the standard of living and quality of life improve."[3] The order of the principles is instructive: private property, the market mechanism, and private enterprise are crucial to creating wealth in the first place. Only after wealth is created does it make any sense at all to think about distributing it.

2. Michael Novak, *Will It Liberate? Questions about Liberation Theology* (Mahwah, N.J.: Paulist, 1986), 46.

3. Kwoh-ting Li, *Economic Transformation of Taiwan (R.O.C.)* (London: Shepheard-Walwyn, 1988), xi.

No workable economy is feasible that fails to take into account the operations of the market. Any economy that violates the principles of a market economy is not only doomed to failure but, even worse, also bound to create conditions in which human liberation becomes even less attainable. Liberation theologians who encouraged people to ignore or reject the market system were, in truth, enemies of the very poor whose cause they claimed to represent.

If liberation theologians are sincere when they talk about economic liberation, they must begin giving more attention to the necessary role wealth creation must play before people can be liberated from poverty. This means that they will have to give greater place to the role of a properly defined capitalism in creating such wealth. Until liberation theologians get their facts and their economics straight, liberation from poverty is the last thing they can provide.

Political liberation. True liberation theology is concerned with more than simply providing economic liberation from poverty. It is also interested in giving people political liberation from tyranny.

Unfortunately, when it comes to political freedom and democracy, the old liberation theologians bear a striking resemblance to the Grand Inquisitor, who promised the people bread while he denied them liberty. The old liberation theologians manifested a disturbing double standard. While they were understandably critical of Right-wing dictatorships (like Chile's, which they wrongly equated with capitalism), their silence about and sometimes explicit support for Left-wing dictatorships (like Cuba, Nicaragua, and Marxist dictatorships in Africa) raises serious doubts about their commitment to democracy. No one can recall hearing so much as a supportive peep from any liberationists for any of the 1989 revolutions in Eastern Europe. The Catholic Church's brave stand against Marxism in Poland is a far more noble example of true liberation theology at work then any specific fruits of the writings of the old liberationists. Many of them revered the tyrant Castro and opposed efforts to bring democracy to Nicaragua.

The inadequacies of the old liberation theology with respect to political liberation are apparent not only in the failure of those thinkers to provide explicit support for political freedom and democracy, but also in their refusal to provide any account of the political structures they hoped to set in place following the revolutions they yearned for. Wise men and women do not encourage revolution without some clear idea of what will occur *after* it. It is helpful to remember Jesus' teaching about the man who was delivered of one evil spirit, only to be taken over by seven spirits more wicked still: "And the final condition of that man is worse than the first" (Matt. 12:45). Beyond the rather elementary matter of declaring for political freedom, it is reasonable to expect liberationists to describe the economic and political institutions they will help set in place after the revolution.

Many older liberation thinkers were shocked when Novak first suggested viewing the American founding fathers as liberation theologians. Providing specific information about the kinds of practical institutions to be established after their revolution was never a problem for the people Novak calls "the liberation theologians of the North." Anyone really interested in learning how to prepare "for the praxis of actual liberation" will learn far more from *The Federalist Papers* than from "any volume of liberation theology written thus far," says Novak, adding, "The first persons to be called, and to call themselves, 'liberals' were so named because they sought *three* liberations. The infant United States was among the first crucibles in which their experiment was tried. They sought liberation from tyranny and torture *in the political sphere*; liberation from the tyranny of poverty *in the economic sphere*; and liberty of conscience, information and ideas *in the religious, cultural and moral sphere*."[4]

Given the sometimes justified anger many Latins feel toward the North, Novak realizes he won't win many friends in the South by talking about the liberation theologians of the North.

4. Novak, *Will It Liberate?* 35, italics original.

But he rightly draws attention to the U.S. founding fathers' important contribution to the cause of liberation.[5] Even though some successors of the founding fathers have sinned against nations in the South, that is no reason to ignore this much earlier and more adequate version of liberation theology.

Spiritual liberation. Since the old liberation theology doesn't offer much real liberation from poverty or tyranny, does it at least offer what we have a right to expect from any Christian message, the message of how people may be delivered from slavery to sin?

The disappointing answer is that most of the old liberation thinkers say absolutely nothing about God's provision for salvation in the death and resurrection of his Son. In fact, many reject beliefs that are essential to the New Testament message of spiritual liberation. They portray Jesus Christ not as the incarnate Son of God but as a human revolutionary concerned to deliver his people from an exclusively earthly oppression. They downplay or deny the divine nature of the Son of God, turning Jesus into an exclusively human liberator. The death of Jesus becomes, in their ideology, a mere symbol of how all Christian revolutionaries should be willing to die as martyrs for their cause.

It is difficult to recognize anything familiar to the long history of Christian orthodoxy in the teachings of the old liberation thinkers. Some have blurred the distinction between the church (the company of redeemed believers) and the world. Some have suggested that the poor are saved simply because they are poor. Others imply that God cares more about the poor than about the rest of humanity, a very large class that includes most of the North American religionists who support liberation ideology with such passion. It is absurd to suggest that all the poor are good and everyone else is evil. It is heresy to state that God's love for people varies in proportion to their wealth.

5. See Ronald H. Nash, *Freedom, Justice and the State* (Lanham, Md.: University Press of America, 1980), chap. 2.

One of the worst examples of how liberationists twist the Scriptures in the service of their ideology is their handling of Luke 4:14–21, probably their most widely used proof-text. In verses 18–19 of this important passage, which defines his mission on earth, Jesus quotes Isaiah 61:1–2 and applies it to his own ministry: "The Spirit of the Lord is on me, because he has anointed me to preach good news to the poor. He has sent me to proclaim freedom for the prisoners and recovery of sight for the blind, to release the oppressed, to proclaim the year of the Lord's favor." Liberationists interpret this passage and Jesus' account of his own mission in exclusively earthly and political terms. They read Luke 4 as a divine endorsement of their politicized version of Christianity.

In truth, Jesus was talking about something different. The prisoners mentioned in Luke 4 are first of all prisoners of sin; the poor he came to deliver are at root spiritually poor because they are devoid of any righteousness that might please God. Jesus' mission was to preach the gospel (God's good news) to all of us who are spiritually bankrupt and deliver us from our enslavement to sin. After all, Jesus came to save his people from their sins (Matt. 1:21). He who commits sin, Jesus taught, is the slave of sin (John 8:34). The only liberation from this enslavement is to be found in the finished work of Christ. "So if the Son sets you free, you will be free indeed" (John 8:36). We were slaves of sin, Paul teaches in Romans 6:17. But thanks to what Jesus did for us in his death and resurrection, we "have been set free from sin" (Rom. 6:18).

This is real liberation for theologians to get excited about! Regrettably, it is a liberation few of the so-called liberation theologians ever talk about. Yet only a society transformed by the saving power of this gospel can bear the fruit of lasting economic prosperity and political liberty. One reason people are poor is that they lack the motivation and ability to change their way of living. Another is that unredeemed rich people oppress them. Still another is that their whole way of viewing the world is inconsistent with the reality God has created and is therefore unproductive. Only the historic, life-transforming gospel can address these and other root problems.

So when Jesus said he came to preach good news to the poor, to proclaim freedom for prisoners, and to release the oppressed, he did indeed imply that the gospel has political and economic implications. But those implications grow out of its spiritual root, and it is as illegitimate to twist the gospel into an exclusively political or economic message as it is to twist it into an exclusively spiritual one. The real good news proclaims spiritual, economic, and political liberty through Christ's transforming power.

The New Liberation Theology

By now, the outline of the new liberation theology should be clear. What it offers is everything the old liberation theology could not deliver because of its captivity to a faulty ideology, a liberal view of biblical inspiration and authority, and a sub-Christian understanding of the church's doctrine. What the old liberation theology did best was practice deceptive advertising. It offered liberation, but it delivered enslavement.

What the poor and oppressed of the world need is more than mere *talk* about liberation, more than simplistic utopian calls for a destructive revolution, the trademark of so many old liberation thinkers. The poor need *caring and thinking* Christians to describe the kinds of economic and political institutions that really deliver the poor from poverty and free the oppressed from tyranny. The best hope for these people is a combination of a free-market economy, limited constitutional government, and the historic, orthodox gospel of Scripture. Together, these provide the foundation for a new liberation theology, a true liberation theology, one that offers genuine hope for spiritual, economic, and political liberation. Every human being in the world has a right to expect self-described Christian theologians to proclaim the New Testament gospel and its message of liberation from sin, poverty, and tyranny. Until liberation theologians begin to do all this, their system will continue to lead not to liberation but to slavery.

With the major arguments of this chapter behind us, it is interesting to see how recent defenders of liberationism have responded to these challenges. The charges of Marxism obviously trouble apologists for liberationism, and there has been a major effort to discredit these claims. Chapter 3 will examine this in greater detail. Gustavo Gutiérrez has begun to pay much more attention to spiritual themes in his recent writings. Hugo Assmann, formerly one of the more radical liberationists, has begun to say nice things about capitalism. One can only hope, despite the absence of much supporting evidence, that many of the other old liberationists will follow their lead.

The old dependency theory has now been widely rejected by older liberationists. Whether that will bear fruit in a more realistic assessment of the causes of poverty in the South remains to be seen. Regrettably, however, there is still almost total silence regarding any careful analysis of economics, especially regarding the debate over capitalism and socialism. We still await any ringing endorsement of democracy from the corps of older liberationists. And it is easy to note their unwillingness to open the can of worms that contains liberationist beliefs about essential Christian doctrines. The next few chapters will explore some of the issues raised in this chapter; the first will be the relationship of liberationism to Marxism.

3

Liberation Theology and Marxism

Many critics of the old liberation theology zero in on the alleged Marxism of its proponents. Many liberationists would love to lay this charge to rest. After all, it would be embarrassing to have subordinated the historic Christian gospel to a secular social and political ideology now repudiated by the Marxist nations of the world! It is difficult enough, these days, to be an atheist Marxist in the United States. How much more trying for one's friends to discover that one has been a "Christian Marxist"!

Yet those attesting the Marxist commitments of the early liberationists include even many sympathetic reporters. For example, Paul Sigmund, professor of government at Princeton University, finds it impossible to deny a relationship between Marxism and the old liberation theology.

> At least at the outset . . . there was a close association between liberation theology and Marxism in the form of the claim that the root cause of the oppression of the poor in Latin America is

"dependent capitalism" and that the way to remove that oppression and to achieve the liberation of the poor is through socialism. Liberation theologians drew on the theory of *dependencia* that had recently been developed in Latin America, and linked it to Marxist theories of the class struggle and exploitation to argue that the church should concern itself with the poor in a specific way by commitment to the (self-) liberation of the poor from dependent capitalism.[1]

Latin American theologian Emilio Nuñez states that most liberation thinkers simply take "for granted that the best economic and social analysis comes from Karl Marx, although they admit that in a certain sense it is necessary to adapt Marxist thought to the concrete situation of Latin America."[2] While not all liberationists were Marxists, most nonetheless were strongly influenced by their study of either Marx himself or his assorted interpreters.

Arthur McGovern admits that in the early writings of almost all liberation thinkers, he finds "an almost unquestioned faith in socialism without a sufficient critique of Marxist-Leninist socialism, which I see as most often destructive of freedom and less than adequate in achieving the economic productivity required for the welfare of society."[3]

According to Kent Hill, director of the Institute for Religion and Democracy, "Even when liberation theologians wish to identify themselves as simply socialist, rather than Marxist, they are frequently willing to cooperate closely with Marxist-Leninists."[4] As we saw in chapter 1, the Vatican's 1984 Instruction on liberation theology criticized the movement for its blind spot about the totalitarian Left's propensity to enslave people.

1. Paul Sigmund, *Liberation Theology at the Crossroads* (New York: Oxford University Press, 1989), 8.

2. Emilio A. Nuñez, *Liberation Theology* (Chicago: Moody, 1985), 28.

3. Arthur F. McGovern, *Liberation Theology and Its Critics: Towards an Assessment* (Maryknoll, N.Y.: Orbis, 1989), xx.

4. Kent R. Hill, "The Discipline of Discernment: Liberation Theology Reconsidered," *Public Eye* (Summer 1988): 14. Hill's article appears on 10–18.

Efforts to Rebut the Charge of Marxism

Two fairly recent books by friends of liberationism include prominent attempts to defuse the charge of Marxism. In his 1987 book *Liberation Theology*, Philip Berryman clearly wants to leave his reader with the impression that whatever Marxist rhetoric may have appeared in liberation writings, it was never meant literally or seriously. There was always a major dichotomy in liberationists' thinking, Berryman argues, a wall between their social theory and what was supposedly most important to them, their "theology." He clearly wishes the issue would go away. Despite his desire to defuse the issue by rewriting history, he is his own worst enemy; he is too partisan to keep his real agenda hidden.

A quick survey of his book reveals his own Marxist sympathies. For example, in one passage he glorifies both Fidel Castro and Camillo Torres, the guerrilla priest.[5] His admiration for Castro's totalitarian rule comes across again late in his book, in a section titled "Cuba a Failure?"[6] Readers can readily guess what Berryman's answer is. Never once does he mention Cuba's almost total economic dependence on the Soviet Union and other communist nations. Neither does he discuss the extent to which Cuba paid for all that aid by sending its sons and daughters to other nations to die fighting for Soviet interests. Nor is he the least enthusiastic about opposing what he calls "authoritarian rule," a euphemism for dictatorship. He thinks freedom may have to be sacrificed "in the pursuit of basic needs."[7] His appeal to needs as a justification for tyranny is identical to arguments denounced by democratic reformers in the Soviet Union and Eastern Europe. In this regard, Berryman sounds strikingly like Fyodor Dostoyevski's Grand Inquisitor.

5. Phillip Berryman, *Liberation Theology* (Philadelphia: Temple University Press, 1987), 17–19.
6. Ibid., 184.
7. Ibid., 142.

In a striking critique of Berryman's allegiances, Hill documents from his book that a major plank of Berryman's position is his resentment to any type of anti-communism.[8] For people like this, Hill notes, the only proper position is a passionate and uncritical anti-anti-communism. "One would think," he writes, "that a theology which centers so fundamentally on compassion for the poor would be at the forefront of the movement to denounce Marxism as one of the most vicious enemies the poor have ever known. . . . Why is it commendable to be concerned about the poor when they are alive, and disgraceful to attack that which has killed them by the millions?"[9] In spite of his protests, then, Berryman's writing actually exemplifies the strong Marxist (indeed, Marxist-Leninist) element in liberation theology.

At first glance, McGovern does a better job defending early liberationists from the charge of Marxism. According to McGovern, "some" liberationists in the early years (the 1970s and early 1980s) did make frequent references to Marxist *analysis*.[10] However, he insists, we should pay less attention to that fact and more to how they used Marxism. They used it, he contends, merely as a *tool* of social analysis even though he quickly admits that the tool was flawed.

McGovern argues that one can use Marxist ideas and language as tools of social analysis without being a Marxist. He seems unaware how problematic this claim is. After all, the elements of Marxist analysis seem to commit those using them to certain unavoidable ways of thinking about the world, particularly about society and economics. For example, if one's "analysis" of a society leads him to believe that people are poor because they have been exploited by rich, powerful, capitalist nations, then the "analysis" of the problem is inseparable from "solutions" that seem indistinguishable from those of more traditional Marxists. Any "analysis" that makes capitalism the vil-

---

8. Ibid., 207.
9. Hill, "The Discipline of Discernment," 10.
10. See McGovern, *Liberation Theology and Its Critics*, xi.

lain seems to require the destruction of "capitalism" as an essential part of the "solution."

Michael Novak points out the second weakness in McGovern's attempt to rescue the early liberationists from the charge of Marxism. The position, Novak argues, fails to do justice to the liberationists' use of the Marxist Sandinistas and the Leninist Castro as models of what the liberationists hoped to accomplish.[11] McGovern's argument is unpersuasive.

A Look at Liberationists' Statements about Marxism

The major problem with recent efforts to hush the debate over the old liberation theology's Marxism is the difficulty these attempts have explaining away truly embarrassing statements in liberationist writings.

There is no need to go any further back than 1971 and the first meeting of Christians for Socialism in Santiago, Chile. The resolutions passed were full of Marxist sentiments. A few examples will give some idea of their content:

> The continued wealth of the rich nations of the North is derived from the exploitation of the poor nations of Latin America. (#2)
>
> The nations of Latin America are maintained in dependent capitalism by rich and powerful national elites who benefit economically from the unjust, oppressive situation. (#4)
>
> The capitalist imperialists seek to prevent the union of Christians and Marxists in order to paralyze the revolutionary process in Latin America. (#21)
>
> Class struggle is the foundation of all correct scientific analysis of society. (#48)
>
> The only solution to the problem of injustice, oppression and domination is that the oppressed nations of Latin

11. See Michael Novak, "Liberation Theology: What's Left," *First Things* (June/July 1991): 12.

America unite to overthrow the power of imperialistic capitalism. (#3)

Socialism cannot be brought about through appeals and denunciations. The exploiting classes must be overthrown. (#11)

As Christians, we do not wish to offer a Christian alternative to the present revolutionary movement, but rather we wish to unite with it. (#8)

Chiefly through Marxist analysis the masses are being awakened to the need to take power. (#32)

The Cuban Revolution and Chilean socialism signal a return to the origins of Marxism and a critique of traditional Marxist dogmatism. (#31)

It is necessary to transform in a radical way all the structures of society in order to create a socialist order. . . . (#7)

Socialism can be achieved only through revolution. (#11)

We have committed ourselves to socialism because after a rigorous and scientific analysis of the situation we have concluded that it is the only effective way to combat imperialism and free us from the slavery of dependence. (#10)[12]

Significantly, both Gustavo Gutiérrez and Hugo Assmann participated in the Santiago meeting.

Gutiérrez's early writings were full of statements that went far beyond any simple use of Marxism as a tool of analysis. He denounced private property, claiming that it resulted from exploitation. He affirmed the class struggle and preached that it was an issue on which neutrality was impossible. Among the central social problems afflicting Latin America, he wrote in 1970,

12. The statements are quoted from the Liberationist Catechism, published by Christians for Socialism in 1972. The statements have been translated by Raymond Hundley in his *Radical Liberation Theology: An Evangelical Response* (Wilmore, Ky.: Bristol, 1987).

is the economical, social, political, and cultural dependence of some peoples on others. That domination involves the complicity of national oligarchies with foreign centers of power which leads to the creation of greater wealth for the few and of greater poverty for the many. To emerge from this situation Latin America needs a social revolution that will radically change the conditions it lives in at present. Today a more or less Marxist inspiration prevails among those groups and individuals who are raising the banner of the continent's revolution. And for many in our continent this liberation will have to pass, sooner or later, through paths of violence.[13]

The Gutiérrez of 1970 sounds as if he can hardly wait for the violence to begin.

Gutiérrez's book *A Theology of Liberation* appeared in 1971.[14] As Sigmund explains, the book argued "that true Christianity involves the overthrow of capitalism and its replacement by a socialism that will overcome the class struggle, the opposition of capital and labor inherent in the private ownership of the means of production."[15] Even though this seemed like an unequivocal call for Latin American Christians to help bring about a socialist revolution, rather incredibly Gutiérrez denied that this was his aim.

In his 1976 book *Christians and Marxists*, Argentinean liberationist and Methodist clergyman José Míguez-Bonino discusses communists like Vladimir Lenin, Mao Tse-tung, and Fidel Castro in the same reverent tones he uses to describe Christian saints and martyrs. He reports that he is moved by "their deep compassion for human suffering and their fierce hatred of oppression and exploitation."[16] No doubt this observation would have surprised the millions of people oppressed, exploited, and murdered at the command of these men!

13. Gustavo Gutiérrez, "Notes from a Theology of Liberation," *Theological Studies* (June 1970): 250.
14. The English edition published by Orbis did not appear until 1973.
15. Sigmund, *Liberation Theology at the Crossroads*, 38.
16. José Míguez-Bonino, *Christians and Marxists* (Grand Rapids: Eerdmans, 1976), 76.

Míguez-Bonino continues, "Indeed, when we observe the process of building a Socialist society in China . . . we see a significant, even preponderant, importance given to the creation of a new man, a solitary human being who places the common good before his own individual interest."[17] The reader must keep in mind that the China he is praising is the China of Mao Tse-tung, a China that the Chinese themselves have since denounced. Sociologist Peter Berger provides a healthy antidote to Míguez-Bonino's ethical short-sightedness when he writes, "*Even if* it were true that Maoism had vanquished hunger among China's poor, this achievement could not morally justify the horrors inflicted by the regime, horrors that entailed the killing of millions of human beings and the imposition of a merciless totalitarian rule on the survivors."[18]

But Míguez-Bonino is not through praising Marxist dictatorships. He writes:

> The political and economic quality and the human value of Socialist revolutions has consistently increased as we move from the USSR to China and Cuba. The social cost has been reduced, the measure of compulsion and repression, particularly in the last case, has been minimized, the welfare of the people has been given at least as much priority as economic development, the disruptive consequences of a blind drive towards industrialization have been avoided. The Chinese and Cuban revolutions have created a sense of participation and achievement on the part of the people and have stimulated a feeling of dignity and moral determination.[19]

One must wonder why Míguez-Bonino was so silent about the millions who died under communist rule in China and in the USSR. Why did he fail to mention the persecution of Christians by these dictators he finds so admirable? Why has he failed to speak out about the slaughter of innocent students in Chi-

17. Ibid.
18. Peter L. Berger, "Underdevelopment Revisited," *Commentary* (July 1984): 43.
19. Míguez-Bonino, *Christians and Marxists*, 77.

na's Tiananmen Square? When it comes to the struggle between the supporters of tyranny and the defenders of liberty, whose side is he on?

Then there are the Nicaraguan liberationist priests Ernesto Cardenal and Miguel D'Escoto. Cardenal, former minister of culture in Nicaragua, believed that "Marxism is the only solution for the world. For me the revolution and the Kingdom of Heaven, mentioned in the Gospel, are the same thing. A Christian should embrace Marxism if he wants to be with God and with men. . . . As Mankind matures, religion will start disappearing slowly until it vanishes completely."[20] This shocking subordination of religious belief to a political agenda by a priest, no less, is echoed by Maryknoll priest D'Escoto, former foreign minister of Nicaragua. D'Escoto once stated, "There are people who call themselves atheists. From the Christian perspective, this is of no great importance. The important thing is the behavior of people. It is the practice not the theory that counts."[21] In 1987, D'Escoto was awarded the Lenin Peace Prize by the Communist Party of the USSR. In accepting the award, he revealed more than he might have liked about his support for Marxism-Leninism:

This prize makes us Nicaraguans come into even closer contact with Lenin, that great personality of your state and of all mankind who is the passionate champion of peace. . . . I believe the Soviet Union is a great torch which emits hope for the preservation of peace on our planet. Always in the vanguard of the overall struggle for peace, the Soviet Union has become the personification of ethical and moral norms in international relations. I admire the revolutionary principles and consistency of the foreign policy of the Communist Party of the fraternal Soviet Union. . . .[22]

20. Cited in Edward Cain, "Nicaraguan Christians Supported the Revolution," *Signposts* 5, 4 (1986): 2.

21. Cited in Cain, "Nicaraguan Christians Supported the Revolution," 2.

22. Cited in "D'Escoto Comes Clean," *Crisis* (January 1988): 2.

D'Escoto's incredible words elicited no objections from supporters of liberation theology.

The Road to Damascus

During the summer of 1989, a strange twenty-eight-page
document, *The Road to Damascus*, was published jointly by the
Catholic Institute for International Relations (London), the
Center of Concern (Washington, D.C.), and Christian Aid
(London). Serving as American distributor of the publication
were Jim Wallis and the Sojourners organization, the radical
Left's chief entry into American evangelicalism. While no
authors of the document are named, signers represent seven
nations: the Philippines, South Korea, Namibia, South Africa,
El Salvador, Nicaragua, and Guatemala. It is hardly a coincidence that all of the signers are Leftists from nations where
Marxist efforts to consolidate Left-wing governments have
been resisted by individuals and nations concerned about the
aid such Marxists have given to proponents of violence and
totalitarianism.

In language designed to assert simultaneously their own virtue and the wickedness of their critics, the writers of *The Road
to Damascus* describe themselves as representatives of a "Christian theology that sides with the poor and oppressed"[23] and
condemn Christians who side "with the oppressor." Whoever
disagrees must, by implication, be an enemy of the poor.

The document's title refers to the apostle Paul's conversion on
the road to Damascus. That conversion transformed Paul from
an enemy and persecutor of Christians to a follower of Christ.
But what the signers and distributors of the Damascus document understood by following Christ differs from what Paul
understood. They use words like "idolatry," "heresy," "apostasy,"
and "blasphemy" to describe failure to support the Marxist
causes they espouse. The good people in this struggle (and pre-

23. *The Road to Damascus: Kairos and Conversion* (published jointly by Catholic Institute for International Relations [London], Center of Concern [Washington, D.C.], and
Christian Aid [London], 1989), 1.

sumably the true followers of Christ) include proponents of liberation theology, black theology, and radical feminist theology. The bad people include any Christians who resist and oppose the efforts of the Christian Marxists. To make certain that the point won't be missed, the document identifies "anti-communist evangelicals" as members of the forces of darkness.[24] In other words, good Christians must be pro-communist; anti-communists are bad Christians. Anti-communist Christians are like Paul before his conversion: enemies of Christ and of the Christian faith. The document calls them to conversion.

The Damascus document is a politically partisan test of what constitutes Christian faithfulness. George Weigel, one of the first to criticize it, objected that it

> offers us nothing less than a political-economic test of Christian fidelity, failing which one is declared, simply, excommunicate: beyond the boundaries of the Body of Christ. Differing views on politics and economics are, in other words, raised above one's affirmation of the classic Christian doctrines (the Trinity, grace, the Incarnation) as the point of division between believers and nonbelievers or, as the document itself puts it, between true Christians and apostates.[25]

Almost as astounding as what the document said was the almost total absence of controversy over it among members of the evangelical and Catholic Left. After all, Richard John Neuhaus pointed out, the document dared to suggest that "a new church has been founded, The People's Church of the Anti-Imperialist Struggle. According to this document, 'the truth of the Christian faith' has little or nothing to do with faith in Christ, Scripture, or the classic creeds, and everything to do with a socio-economic analysis of class struggle. The creedal key . . . is 'the preferential option for the poor.'"[26] Neuhaus

24. Ibid.
25. George Weigel, "Still Blind, On the Road to Damascus," *American Purpose* (November 1989): 65.
26. Richard John Neuhaus, "Ambushed on the Road to Damascus," *First Things* (April 1990): 66.

branded shameful the silence of supposedly responsible Christians in the U.S. who have tried to act as if the document never existed and wasn't distributed by the Sojourners.

It must be remembered that *The Road to Damascus* appeared before any of these pro-communist "Christians" even imagined that anti-communism would become fashionable in the Soviet Union and the People's Republic of China. Little did they dream that anti-communism would become the cutting edge of history in the next few months. All of this makes Weigel's criticism more fitting:

> The time is long past when those who most loudly proclaim their "preferential option for the poor" should be given the benefit of the doubt. The world has learned some things about poverty and wealth, development and underdevelopment, these last few decades or so. We have learned that human resources and capital are as important, and probably more important, than natural resources. We have learned that market-oriented economies are far more likely to raise the poor's standard of living than state-centered or command economies. We have learned that the entrepreneurial energies of the people of the Third World are being strangled by a thick net of mercantilist and modern statist regulations. We have learned that postindependence dictators in the Third World are often more corrupt than their former colonial masters. We have learned that aggregate amounts of foreign aid are no index of successful development in the recipient nation. And we have learned that when people are actually given the choice, they inevitably opt for the kinds of economies that allow them to function as free economic actors.[27]

And yet, Weigel continues, "the sponsors and authors of the Damascus Document seem wholly innocent of all this."

> Twenty years ago there may have been an excuse for such extraordinary ignorance of empirical reality. But now there is no excuse. One is ignorant of these things either because one is cul-

27. Weigel, "Still Blind, On the Road to Damascus," 66–67.

pably lazy and not paying very much attention or because one finds the truth ideologically unsettling. In either case, the result is bad news for the poor, for whom one has supposedly "opted."[28]

This powerful indictment applies not only to the signers and sponsors of the Damascus Document but also to those outdated liberationists who still cling to the socialist and revolutionary dreams of the past and to their utopian fellow-travellers in American Christendom.

What the last few pages of this chapter make clear is that many spokesmen for the old liberation theology were involved with far more than an innocent flirtation with Marxist social analysis. They were engaged in a totally uncritical, passionate commitment to a total Marxist agenda. In the next section, we will examine one final attempt to distance liberationists from Marxism.

Five Alleged Differences Between Liberationism and Marxism

Arthur McGovern has identified what he thinks are five major ways in which liberation theologians interact with Marxism.[29]

(1) Marxist ideas function primarily as tools. Liberationists select only those ideas they find useful without worrying about the broader system orthodox Marxists insist is essential to their enterprise. In other words, the appearance of Marxist ideas and language in liberationists' writings does not mean they are committed to the usual Marxist system.

While there may be some liberationists for whom this observation is correct, it hardly fits the words and ideas noted earlier in this chapter. Neither can McGovern completely succeed in claiming that whatever radical statements remain belong to an

28. Ibid., 67.

29. McGovern draws these points from Otto Maduro's unpublished manuscript "The Desacralization of Marxism within Latin American Liberation Theology." See McGovern, *Liberation Theology and Its Critics*, 146.

early stage of liberation thinking. *The Road to Damascus*, published during the very summer when the communist leaders of China massacred thousands of students and just a few months before the revolutions of 1989 rocked European communism, proves that proponents of hard-core, utopian-style Marxism still parade under the liberation banner. McGovern's first claim simply ignores too much evidence to the contrary.

(2) Liberationists are too smart to believe the usual Marxist hoopla about Marx's supposed discovery of the iron-clad laws that supposedly govern history and make the triumph of Marxism inevitable. On this point, we think, McGovern is on more solid ground. This important element of Marxism-Leninism is difficult to find in major writings of older liberationists.

(3) Liberationists find the usual Marxist attack on religion inadequate. The Marxist critique is, McGovern claims, a white, European, male chauvinistic put-down of the poor as people deluded by other-worldly aspirations. It would be difficult to see how the thinkers covered in this book could continue to maintain their credentials as liberation *theologians* if they surrendered to something as simplistic as Marx's attack on religion. At the same time, however, this might be a good time to turn back a few pages and reread the statements by Sandinistas Cardenal and D'Escoto, who sound as if liberation theology may be only a stage on the road to a higher level of consciousness in which religion becomes dispensable.

(4) Liberation thinkers repudiate efforts of Marxist-Leninists to impose a small group of elitist leaders over the poor. Such elitism only enhances the dependency of the poor. In McGovern's words, "Liberation theology believes that the poor must be agents of their own destiny, using their own creativity, initiative, and leadership."[30]

This interesting statement sounds surprisingly like a thesis we usually associate with liberationist critic Novak. McGovern is certainly correct when he notes that liberationist support for any kind of statism that makes the masses subject to the will of

30. McGovern, *Liberation Theology and Its Critics*, 146.

a small cadre of elitists is incompatible with liberation thought. But while he assumes that the older liberationists recognized this inconsistency, the textual evidence shows that they did not. While we applaud even their belated realization that a true liberation theology *must*, on pain of inconsistency, support not only democracy but also the decentralization of economic power inherent in true capitalism, the realization is in fact recent. Furthermore, the authors and sponsors of *The Road to Damascus*, regrettably, still advocate a statism in which the mass of the poor must be led by the enlightened elitists whose views dominate that document.

(5) Finally, McGovern writes, "liberation theologians reject all models of authoritarian government including Marxist models. . . . liberation theology stresses participation and shared leadership."[31] While we can applaud McGovern's insistence on this point and hope that it does indeed become policy for all future liberation thinkers, we have already seen too many statements that falsify McGovern's claim. Statements to the effect that liberationists reject authoritarian governments are hardly consistent with liberationists' effusive praise for Soviet, Chinese, and Cuban dictatorships.

At times, one suspects that writers like McGovern would prefer that we simply forget the shameful statements of the past and trust that responsible liberationists in the future will show more sense about Marxism than did earlier ones. But it is hard to forget that years of uncritical infatuation with Marxism cruelly postponed what liberationists said was their ultimate objective: true liberation for the poor and oppressed peoples of the world. The utopian Marxists in the liberation movement must bear the blame for the harm they did to their cause and to the poor they claimed to represent.

What About Neo-Marxism?

A chapter about Marxism in a book on liberationism could not be complete without some discussion of Neo-Marxism.

31. Ibid.

The world does contain different versions of Marxism.
Marxism-Leninism has received the bulk of our attention thus
far. Lenin's interpretation of Marxism triumphed in Russia,
China, and Cuba, and then was imposed forcibly on whatever
other nations were unfortunate enough to become captive to
Soviet imperialism. Marxism-Leninism made atheistic materi-
alism an essential part of the Marxist ideology; it also turned
Marxism into an engine of totalitarianism. There is no doubt
but that the liberation movement has had its share of Marxist-
Leninists in its ranks.

But the Leninist label never really fit people like Gutiérrez
and others, however sloppy their thinking. What if many of the
old liberationists really *meant* to espouse Neo-Marxism? Would
this somehow defuse the entire issue?

Hardly. The plausibility of this argument declines considerably in light of two fatal flaws in Neo-Marxism itself. First, the
developers of Neo-Marxism advocated their own kind of totalitarianism. Second, Neo-Marxism depends on an utterly
untenable reading of Marx's writings.

Neo-Marxism and totalitarianism. The major representatives
of Neo-Marxism have been Herbert Marcuse, Erich Fromm,
and Antonio Gramsci. Their influence can be seen in liberationists like Gutiérrez, Assmann, José Porfirio Miranda, and
Juan Luis Segundo.[32]

Marcuse was an unsparing critic of all advanced industrial
societies, especially the United States. The details of his critique
are less important than why the people who live in these corrupt societies don't do something about it. His answer was that
they can't. Marx believed that the workers would carry the rev-

32. See Gustavo Gutiérrez, *A Theology of Liberation: History, Politics and Salvation*,
trans. Caridad Inda and John Eagleson (Maryknoll, N.Y.: Orbis, 1973), 31–32, 233;
José Porfirio Miranda, *Marx and the Bible: A Critique of the Philosophy of Oppression*, trans.
John Eagleson (Maryknoll, N.Y.: Orbis, 1974), chap. 5; Hugo Assmann, *Theology for a
Nomad Church*, trans. Paul Burns (Maryknoll, N.Y.: Orbis, 1976), 79; and Juan Luis
Segundo, *The Liberation of Theology*, trans. John Drury (Maryknoll, N.Y.: Orbis, 1976),
52–53. For a critical account of Gramsci by one of the authors of this book, see Ronald
H. Nash, *The Closing of the American Heart* (Richardson, Tex.: Probe, 1990), 145–46.

olution. But Marcuse thought that Marx failed to see how the workers would become part of the establishment. Marcuse believed that the worker in an advanced industrial society becomes corrupted by the affluence of the society until he has the same values as the oppressor class.

According to Marcuse, modern technology in societies like the U.S. eliminates dissent and conflict that might arise in less advanced societies by raising false needs and providing false satisfaction. It enslaves people by deceiving them into thinking that it gives them what they really want: better homes and appliances, faster cars, more leisure and luxury. In effect, Americans are so completely dominated, controlled, preconditioned, indoctrinated, and brainwashed that they cannot even recognize their bondage. People become so obsessed by the gadgets they want to possess and consume that they forget that this obsession might destroy them. The possibility of anyone in any advanced industrial society rising up against the hand that feeds him is faint, perhaps nonexistent.

Marcuse attacked this false mass contentment by claiming that the goods produced by capitalism provide false satisfaction. First the system manipulates people into wanting things; then it seduces them into buying them; then, through devices like advertising, it increases these wants until the desire to consume becomes compulsive, irrational, and inhuman. The belief of the average woman that she is happy only shows how total her bondage is. The things that make us think we are happy (electric can openers, indoor toilets, diet colas, boysenberry-flavored breakfast cereals) are the chains that bind us. Marcuse *knew* the members of a capitalist society were really unhappy. It made no difference if someone identified with her needs and believed they were hers. He knew her needs were the false product of a repressive society.

What we really need, he claimed, is to free ourselves from false consciousness and its artificial needs and gain true consciousness and its recognition of true needs. We need to become a new type of human being that cannot be seduced by affluence.

It is not enough, however, for Marcuse to argue that humans must free themselves from the oppressive influence of false needs imposed by a repressive society; he should also have explained *how* this could be done. More importantly, he should have shown, given his analysis of our lost estate in the modern advanced industrial society, that the attainment of liberation and autonomy is possible. He may have backed himself into a corner with no way out. As he put it, "How can the people who have been the object of effective and productive domination by themselves create the conditions of freedom?"[33] His problem stemmed from his own claim that there was no way for the system to correct itself because it was impossible for those dominated by it ever to free themselves from it.

Two additional problems with Marcuse's theory seem to make liberation impossible. First, Marcuse argued that social change could not take place through democratic means because democracy contributes to the plight of society by lulling people into decisions that are against their best interests. Advanced industrial societies like the United States appear tolerant of minority views because they know that those views cannot have any effect. People are not really free when they vote and make political decisions because, according to Marcuse, all who start out under the domination of a repressive society are preconditioned receptacles; they are incapable of criticizing the society or even of heeding a legitimate criticism.

Second, this led Marcuse to his doctrine of "Repressive Tolerance."[34] Because American society is in such peril, he came to believe that the suspension of free speech and free assembly are justified. After all, there is no real value to freedom of speech; it only insures the propagation of lies. Truth is carried by revolutionary minorities like Marcuse's disciples! Therefore, tolerance should be withdrawn from all who disagree with Mar-

33. Herbert Marcuse, *One-Dimensional Man* (Boston: Beacon, 1964), chap. 1.

34. Described in one of three essays by Herbert Marcuse, R. P. Wolff, and Barrington Moore, Jr., *A Critique of Pure Tolerance* (Boston: Beacon, 1967). Another source for many of Marcuse's ideas reported here was *An Essay on Liberation* (Boston: Beacon, 1969).

cuse and extended only to those who make what he called the
Great Refusal. Social change can be brought about not by democratic legality but by extra-democratic rebellion. Marcuse
wanted to replace democratically supported elites with an elite
of his own choosing. Oddly enough, he admitted that even if his
totalitarian measures were put into practice and his followers
succeeded in destroying existing society, he could not be sure
what would follow.[35]

The questions raised by Marcuse's theory are obvious: How
does his elite free itself from the conditioning that blinds everyone else? And who will provide deliverance from the repressive-
ness of his elite? Such considerations have led several interpreters of Marcuse to see signs of a neo-Nazi mentality in his
position.[36]

While the first difficulty Marcuse saw in achieving liberation
was the failure of the democratic process, the second was the
powerlessness of critical social theory to criticize. The very categories of critical theory were developed within the structure of
the system. Furthermore, those who might offer the criticism
are preconditioned by the system. And finally, those who might
otherwise be influenced by a criticism of their society are so
brainwashed that they cannot appreciate the force of or understand the nature of the criticism. Thus, there is no one to offer
the critique, no one to understand it, and no critical theory in
terms of which the needed critique can be given. Things indeed
look hopeless. But for whom? Perhaps Marcuse created a
greater problem for himself than for capitalism.

Just when things looked hopeless, Marcuse, who wrote in the
late 1960s, began to see signs of the Great Refusal all over the
place: the revolutions in Vietnam, Cuba, and China (hardly
bastions of Neo-Marxism, these Marxist-Leninist domains!);
guerrilla activities in Latin America; strains in the fortress of
corporate capitalism; stirrings among ghetto populations; and,

35. See Marcuse, Wolff, and Moore, *Critique of Pure Tolerance*, 87.
36. See Dale Vree, "A Comment on 'Some Irrational Sources of Opposition to the
Market System,'" in *Capitalism: Sources of Hostility*, ed. Ernest van den Haag (New Roch-
elle, N.Y.: Epoch, 1979), 155–56.

last but not least, student uprisings. He became both a prophet and a hero to the radical Left and New Left movements on America's college campuses.

But there was a huge and embarrassing hole right in the middle of Marcuse's argument. How, given the total domination of the repressive society, was all this opposition possible? Since Marcuse had claimed that all people living in advanced industrial societies are controlled, manipulated, and brainwashed to the extent that they think they are happy, are unable to see their society's faults, and are unable to appreciate criticisms of their society, *Marcuse's thesis turns out to be self-defeating.* Why? Because no one, including himself, could have obtained knowledge of the thesis! Even granting that his books could be the result of some kind of miracle, no one else, according to his theory, could have understood him.

Marcuse's theory continues to exercise a bizarre hold over many "intellectuals" in the United States. But in the constant interaction between the old liberationists and the propagandists of New Left ideas in the North, this strange assortment of Neo-Marxist ideas continues to bounce around in the loosely constructed systems of old liberationists. It continues to be one of the mysteries of late-twentieth-century thought how so many intellectuals can be so uncritically captive to a set of ideas that turn out to be logically self-defeating. Equally amazing is the number of these ideologues who remain seemingly blind to the totalitarian implications of Marcuse's position.

Neo-Marxism, alienation, and Marx's early unpublished writings. Neo-Marxism differs from Leninism and other versions of Marxism in terms of the importance it attaches to a number of Marx's early unpublished manuscripts.[37] Several things should be noted about these early writings. (1) Marx never tried to publish them. Since he never hesitated to publish many writings of seemingly little importance, some have concluded that he

---

37. These manuscripts, along with a helpful introduction, can be found in Karl Marx, *Early Writings*, trans. and ed. T. B. Bottomore (New York: McGraw-Hill, 1964).

regarded these early scribblings as unworthy of publication. (2) Marx wrote these early manuscripts four years before he and Friedrich Engels published the *Manifesto of the Communist Party* in 1848. In the opinion of many Marxist scholars, he wrote these early manuscripts before he himself even became a Marxist! (3) The early manuscripts were not published (in German) until 1932. Publication of English translations would come years later.

The most important doctrine contained in the early manuscripts is Marx's teaching about alienation. This doctrine is the trademark of Neo-Marxism. Marx is thought to have identified four different but related forms of worker alienation.

First, capitalism causes workers to become alienated from what they produce. The details of this point can be learned by rereading the previous section of this chapter on Marcuse. Because the capitalist system supposedly creates false needs and provides false satisfactions, it manipulates workers into wanting things and then seduces them into buying them. Workers become dominated and controlled by the things they are forced to make.

Second, workers are estranged from the labor process itself. Of course, many men and women do hate their jobs. Third, workers under capitalism become alienated from other men and women. Fourth, workers finally become alienated from themselves. But all three of these phenomena are as easily observed in socialist as in capitalist nations.

For Neo-Marxists, Sidney Hook explains,

> Marxism is not primarily a system of sociology or economics, but a philosophy of human liberation. It seeks to overcome human alienation, to emancipate man from repressive social institutions, especially economic institutions that frustrate his true nature, and to bring him into harmony with himself, his fellow men, and the world around him so that he can both overcome his estrangements and express his true essence through creative freedom.[38]

38. Sidney Hook, *Marxism and Beyond* (Totowa, N.J.: Rowman and Littlefield, 1983), 46.

The development of Neo-Marxism obviously had to await the publication of Marx's early writings, an event that took place in 1932. In the early 1930s, the early manuscripts seemed to reveal a Marx quite different from the official Marx of Stalinism. For people weary of or frightened by the ruthless tyranny of Joseph Stalin, it was possible to appeal to the authority of the early Marx in defense of individual human dignity and freedom, or so some people claimed.

The plausibility of Neo-Marxism depends to a great extent on the place Marx's early unpublished writings should have in any correct understanding of his system. Critics of Neo-Marxism have tended to dismiss both the early writings and their teaching about alienation, denying that they are essential to the real Marx.

But according to Neo-Marxism, Marx's later writings should be interpreted in light of these early writings. According to Fromm, "[I]t is impossible to understand Marx's concept of socialism and his criticism of capitalism as developed except on the basis of his concept of man which he developed in his early writings."[39] Neo-Marxists believe his position remained basically the same from his early 1844 writings through his later publications. The key that unlocks the meaning of the entire system lies hidden in the early unpublished manuscripts. Neo-Marxists largely ignore the teachings for which Marx became most famous, namely, the labor theory of value, dialectical materialism, and the class struggle. The new Marx is a philosopher whose primary concern is to draw attention to human estrangement caused by an oppressive society.

While some interpreters of Marx think his later writings provide his most important teachings, still others believe that the early and later writings contain two different systems that are quite incompatible. The supposed humanism of the early Marx is not germane to the concerns of the later Marx, these critics of Neo-Marxism argue.

39. Erich Fromm, *Marx's Concept of Man* (New York: Ungar, 1961), 79.

Hook places the issue of the early manuscripts on the table when he observes: "The most fantastic interpretations have been placed on these [early] groping efforts of Marx towards intellectual maturity."[40] One of the more jarring implications of the Neo-Marxist interpretation is that no one really understood Marx until 1932, the year his early manuscripts were finally published. Even though he devoted twenty years of hard labor to *Capital*, and even though it was a book for which he sacrificed almost everything in his life, including health and family, the Neo-Marxist version of Marx turns *Capital*, in the words of Robert Tucker, into "an intellectual museum piece . . . whereas the sixteen-page manuscript of 1844 on the future of aesthetics, which he probably wrote in a day and never even saw fit to publish, contains much that is still significant."[41]

Hook is not alone in observing that there are too many differences in focus and emphasis between the early and later Marx to see the former as crucial to understanding the latter:

> The old Marx is interested in the mechanics or organics of capitalism as an economic system, in politics as the theatre of clashing economic interests, and in the theory and practice of revolution. He is so impatient of the rhetoric of piety and morality that he sometimes gives the impression of a thinker who had no moral theory whatsoever, and whose doctrines logically do not allow for considered moral judgment. The new Marx, barely out of his intellectual swaddling clothes, sounds like *nothing but* a moralist. . . .[42]

Critics of Neo-Marxism go on to argue that the notion of alienation practically disappears from Marx's later writings. Attempts to locate something like the early doctrine of alienation in passages where the mature Marx mentions psychological phenomena are persuasive only to those already committed

40. Sidney Hook, "Marxism in the Western World," in *Marxist Ideology in the Contemporary World* (New York: Praeger, 1966), 16.

41. Robert Tucker, *Philosophy and Myth in Karl Marx* (Cambridge: Harvard University Press, 1961), 235.

42. Hook, "Marxism in the Western World," 27.

to the Neo-Marxist interpretation. Passages like *Capital* 1.1.4
are cited by some advocates of Neo-Marxism to show that even
though the later Marx did not use the same language one finds
in the unpublished writings (such as the term *alienation*), he
continued to refer to the concept. But such claims depend on a
superficial reading of Marx that ignores important differences
in the stages of his thought. There are obvious inconsistencies
between the early doctrine of alienation and the later passages
supposed to express the same view in different language. The
early Marx saw alienation as the *cause* and private property as
the *effect*. But the later Marx, having done a 180-degree turn,
saw the psychological phenomena Neo-Marxists now call
alienation by other names as *effects* of private ownership of the
means of production. In other words, the later Marx treated
private property as the cause of what, in the mature writings, is
supposed to be the equivalent of alienation in the early writings.
The two positions are totally inconsistent.

But things get worse for the Neo-Marxist view. Marx actually repudiated his early doctrine of alienation. Daniel Bell
regards efforts to discover a radical analysis of society in the
early Marx as an attempt to create a new myth to buttress
attempts to use Marx's name and authority in support of new
causes. While he agrees that these views of alienation may be
found in the early Marx, he also points out that they cannot be
found in the mature Marx, who, in effect, repudiated the idea
of alienation.[43] Even in *The Communist Manifesto*, Hook argues,
"Marx explicitly disavows the theory of alienation as 'metaphysical rubbish,' as a linguistic Germanic mystification of
social phenomena described by French social critics."[44]

If scholars like Hook and Bell are correct, if the mature Marx
really did abandon his earlier immature opinions on alienation,
then all of "Christian Marxism" rests on a questionable interpretation of questionable writings that are the basis of a questionable theory that, in all likelihood, Marx himself repudiated.

43. See Daniel Bell, "The 'Rediscovery' of Alienation," *The Journal of Philosophy* 56
(1959): 933–52.

44. Hook, *Marxism and Beyond*, 48.

The Christian use of Marxism, it appears, is a system built on quicksand.

Although they clearly demonstrated their enthusiasm for Marxism throughout the 1970s and well into the 1980s, liberation theologians now seem anxious to get people to forget that they did. Liberation apologists sometimes appear intent on rewriting history in their desire to obscure the past. But the 1989 publication of *The Road to Damascus* makes it clear that hard-core, utopian Marxists are still around. At the same time, older liberationists like Gutiérrez and Assmann, the latter one of the more intractable of the early liberation Marxists, appear to be Marxists no longer. While advocates of the new liberation theology set forth in this book welcome these changing attitudes toward Marxism, we wonder why the changes are so tepid and are not accompanied by some criticism of the radicals. Finally, to whatever extent older liberationists supported positions associated with it, Neo-Marxism has always been highly problematic. Support for totalitarianism has always been at its very core. Uncritical acceptance of the position put ideologically committed Leftists in the untenable position of having to defend beliefs that the mature Marx rejected.

However ambiguous the old liberation theology was and still is regarding Marxism, there is no equivocation on the part of the new liberation theology. It rejects totally any resort to Marx for ideas helpful to the world's poor and oppressed peoples. Even more, the new liberation theologians condemn Marxism because Marx's heirs have killed millions of people in this century and brought unspeakable misery to millions more.

4

Liberation Theology and Capitalism

All of the old liberation thinkers were committed social-ists. As Arthur McGovern admits, "I have yet to find any lib-eration theologians who do not favor some kind of social-ism."[1] José Míguez-Bonino summarizes the attitude old liberationists had toward capitalism when he writes, "[T]he basic ethos of capitalism is definitely anti-Christian: it is the maximizing of economic gain, the raising of man's grasping impulse, the idolizing of the strong, the subordination of man to economic production. . . . In terms of their basic ethos, Christians must criticize capitalism radically, in its fundamental intention."[2] For Míguez-Bonino and others who think as he does or at least as he once did, capitalism is un-Christian or anti-Christian because it allegedly gives a predominant place to greed and other un-Christian values.

1. Arthur F. McGovern, *Liberation Theology and Its Critics: Towards an Assessment* (Maryknoll, N.Y.: Orbis, 1989), 148.
2. José Míguez-Bonino, *Christians and Marxists* (Grand Rapids: Eerdmans, 1976), 115.

It is alleged to increase poverty and the misery of the poor while it enriches a few at the expense of the many. Socialism, in contrast, is supposed to be the economic system of people who really care for the less fortunate members of society. It is the economics of compassion.

Making a positive case for capitalism to people who think this way isn't easy. Part of the challenge is showing socialists that their judgment is based on a caricature of capitalism.

Liberation thinkers equate capitalism with the economic and political systems of the industrialized Western nations in general and of the United States in particular. But what if these turned out not to be capitalist? What if these economic and political systems, with all their problems, turned out to be variations of the same kind of statism that liberationists have, at least until now, wished to impose on the nations of Latin America? The religious Left seems unable to grasp this line of argument, even though it has been stated in several recent books.[3]

Moreover, liberationists equate capitalism with the economic structures in Latin America that have brought poverty and misery to the people Latin liberationists claim to represent. But what if they are also wrong on this point? What if Latin America has *never* been capitalist? What if the economic systems of the South that liberationists hate with such passion are not capitalist but statist and interventionist systems that differ only by degree from the economic structures the liberation socialists believe are the solution for the economic ills of the South? Clearly, there is plenty here that demands deeper thinking about economics than one can find in any writing of the old liberation theology.

3. See the following by Ronald H. Nash: *Freedom, Justice and the State* (Lanham, Md.: University Press of America, 1980); *Social Justice and the Christian Church* (Lanham, Md.: University Press of America, 1992 [1st ed., 1983]); *Poverty and Wealth: The Christian Debate over Capitalism* (Richardson, Tex.: Probe, 1992 [1st ed., 1986]); and "The Christian Choice between Capitalism and Socialism," in *Liberation Theology*, ed. Ronald H. Nash (Grand Rapids: Baker, 1988), 45–67.

Three Economic Systems

Three relatively simple steps could help any reasonable and open-minded person gain a perspective from which to begin sorting these things out. The first step is to recognize that there are actually three economic systems competing for attention in the world. In addition to capitalism and socialism, which still require definition, there is a third system called interventionism or the mixed economy. The relationship among these three systems is pictured in figure 1.

Figure 1
The Three Economic Systems

Capitalism	Interventionism	Socialism

0   100

The second step is to see that our three words denote not single, fixed positions but a variety of options along a continuum. It is best to treat our three terms as umbrella words that cover a variety of positions. The dominant feature that determines whether a nation's economy is socialist, interventionist, or capitalist is the degree of economic freedom its citizens enjoy. Generally speaking, as one moves along the continuum from socialism to capitalism, one finds the following: the more freedom a socialist system allows, the closer it comes to being a form of interventionism; the more freedom an interventionist system allows, the closer it is to capitalism. The real issue in the dispute among these three positions is the degree of economic freedom each allows. The crux is the degree to which human beings are permitted to exercise their own choices in the economic sphere of life.

Recent events in China and the Soviet Union show that a nation's economy can move quickly along this continuum. In the mid-1970s, when China could not feed its own people, the Chinese economy operated very close to the extreme right (socialist) side of the continuum. During the 1980s, the totalitarian rulers of

China experimented with various measures allowing greater economic freedom, as in agriculture. China's economy moved toward the center of the continuum (interventionism). The result was astounding. Introducing market incentives into agriculture improved China's food production so dramatically that it was able to export food. But while all this was happening, China's communist leaders forgot one important thing: that once people get a taste of liberty, they want more. It is impossible to separate economic freedom from political freedom. Many tragedies occurred in Beijing's Tiananmen Square during the summer of 1989. One was the decision by China's dictators to resist the popular move to democracy, a drift that threatened their privileges and power. When those rulers ordered the army to shoot the brave young students and workers in Tiananmen Square, China did more than say no to political liberty; it also stopped its progress toward economic freedom and prosperity.

As the events of August 1991 reveal, reform-minded people in the Soviet Union have been attempting to nudge that nation toward greater economic freedom. The attempted coup was an effort by hard-line communists interested primarily in preserving their privileges and power to put an end to this drift away from the extreme socialist end of the continuum.

The third step toward sorting out liberation theology's confusion over economic systems is to recognize that the economies of the United States and the industrialized nations of the West (Germany, Britain, France, Canada, and so on) are really interventionist, not capitalist. In each case, cleverly devised political-economic structures allow the powerful modern state and the power structure of elitists and insiders (including many powerful businessmen) to interfere with the market economy to gain special privileges for themselves. The rich and powerful in the West have successfully persuaded many people that governmental tinkering with the economy is designed primarily to rectify injustices of the market system. The truth, however, is the opposite.[4]

4. For a detailed analysis of the claims of this paragraph and a lengthy defense, see Nash, *Poverty and Wealth*.

Many complaints about economic policies and conditions in the United States are justified. But when the policies are interventionist, it is hardly fair to blame them or the problems they cause on capitalism. When interventionist measures lead, as they always do, to severe economic distortions,[5] interventionist economists never admit that the difficulties result from their attempts to tamper with the economy. The problems result, they complain, from insufficient intervention. In this ingenious but dishonest way, interventionists cite the failures of interventionism as reasons for even greater degrees of interventionism.

Whenever capitalism is blamed for the problems of Latin America, the same confusion between capitalism and interventionism is at work. None of the national economies of Latin America is now or ever has been capitalist. All of them are examples of extensive statist interference with market processes far more extensive than the intervention in the West. If liberation theologians want to condemn the economic structures of Latin America, they should turn their wrath on interventionism, not on capitalism.

Capitalism

One dominant feature of capitalism (as opposed to interventionism) is economic freedom, the right of people to exchange things voluntarily, free from force, fraud, and theft. Capitalism is more than this, of course, but its concern with free exchange is obvious. Socialism, in contrast, seeks to replace the freedom of the market with a group of central planners who exercise control over essential market functions. There are degrees of socialism as there are degrees of capitalism in the real world.

5. Major examples of economic interventionism include wage and price controls (or subsidies) and tariffs, which cause shortages or surpluses of labor and products, and manipulation of the money supply (which causes rising or falling nominal prices and related distortions of the information communicated by the market). Intervention is an attempt by government to alter the terms of economic exchange in ways that benefit some at the expense of others. The consequences of interventionism include greater unemployment than would otherwise have been the case, deeper periods of economic reversal than would otherwise have been the case, and inflation. See Nash, *Poverty and Wealth*, chaps. 11–14.

But basic to any form of socialism is distrust of or contempt for the market process and the desire to replace the freedom of the market with some form of centralized control.

An excellent way to grasp the essential difference between capitalism and socialism is a distinction, drawn most recently by economist Walter Williams, between the two ways in which exchanges may occur. Williams calls them *the peaceful means of exchange* and *the violent means of exchange.*

Peaceful exchange may be summed up in the promise, "If you do something good for me, then I'll do something good for you." Understood correctly, capitalism epitomizes peaceful exchange. People enter a market exchange because they believe the exchange is good for them. They take advantage of an opportunity to obtain something they value more in exchange for something they value less. Capitalism then should be understood as a voluntary system of relationships that uses the peaceful means of exchange. Because economic interventionism uses the coercive power of the state, it cannot model the peaceful means of exchange.

But exchange can also take place by means of force and violence. Violent exchange may be summed up in the threat, "Unless you do something good for me, I'll do something bad to you." This turns out to be the controlling principle of socialism. Socialism means far more than centralized control of the economic process. It entails the introduction of coercion into economic exchanges to facilitate the goals of the elite, the central planners. One of the great ironies of Christian socialism is that its proponents in effect demand that the state get out its weapons and force people to fulfill the demands of Christian love. Even if we fail to notice any other contrast between capitalism and socialism, we already have a major difference to relate to the biblical ethic. One system stresses voluntary and peaceful exchange, the other depends on coercion and violence.

The "voluntary socialism" many Christian socialists seem to support is actually a contradiction in terms. Voluntarily sharing goods and the tasks of a community does not make a set of economic arrangements socialist. Within the model of capitalism recommended by this book, groups of people are perfectly free to establish communes and communities that observe common ownership so long as people participate in these arrangements voluntarily. The catch for these communities is that if they are going to have economic relationships with individuals or communities beyond their own narrow boundaries, they will have to observe market principles and arrangements.[6]

Whenever a Christian socialist talks about "voluntary socialism," all he has done is form either a utopian ideal of a voluntary community and call it socialism, or a utopian ideal of a socialist community and call it voluntary. But calling something socialism does not make it socialist. Neither does calling something voluntary make it voluntary. In reality, the two are mutually exclusive. Self-styled Christian socialists cannot explain how their system will work without free markets, and they simply ignore the massive amounts of coercion required to get any truly socialist system started and keep it going. Whatever else socialism is, it means centralized control of the economy by force. Socialism epitomizes violent exchange.

A Closer Look at Capitalism

We have already explained capitalism as a system of voluntary human relationships in which people exchange by peaceful means. It is time to add more detail to this general picture.

Capitalism is not economic anarchy. It recognizes several necessary conditions for the kinds of voluntary relationships it recommends. One is the existence of inherent human rights, such as the right to make decisions, the right to be free, the right to hold property, and the right to exchange what one owns for something else. Capitalism also presupposes a system of morality. It does not encourage people to do anything they want. It recognizes definite limits, moral and otherwise, to the ways in which people should exchange.

6. For an explanation of markets and how they operate, see Nash, *Poverty and Wealth*, chap. 5.

Capitalism should be regarded as a system of voluntary relationships within a framework of laws that protect people's rights against force, fraud, theft, and violations of contracts. "Thou shalt not steal" and "Thou shalt not lie" are part of the underlying moral constraints of the system. Economic exchanges can hardly be voluntary if one participant is coerced, deceived, defrauded, or robbed. People who condemned the "capitalism" of the Philippines under Ferdinand Marcos or of Nicaragua under Anastasio Somoza had no idea what they were talking about. The corruption deserved condemnation, but the system was not capitalism.

Christians can easily understand why it is so difficult in the real world for economic systems to move very far toward the capitalist end of the continuum. Deviations from the market ideal occur because of defects in human nature. People naturally crave security and guaranteed success, conditions not found readily in a free market. Genuine competition always carries with it the possibility of failure and loss. Consequently, the preference for security leads people to avoid competition whenever possible, encourages them to operate outside the market, and induces them to subvert the market process through behavior that is often questionable and dishonest. But the primary way in which sinful human beings seek to avoid the uncertainties of the market is by finding ways to get the government on their side, by persuading the state to grant them special privileges. This is why national economies that are called capitalist are in fact examples of interventionism. Propagandists for interventionism justify governmental intrusion into the market on the grounds that it is necessary to achieve fairness and break down the power of small groups who have garnered inordinate degrees of economic power. The truth is quite different, however. Interventionism occurs when government alters the terms of trade in ways that benefit some at the expense of others.[7]

7. It is impossible to say everything we would like at this point. For a detailed analysis of these claims, see Nash, *Poverty and Wealth*.

Capitalism often is accused of making it easier for vast concentrations of wealth and power to be vested in the hands of private individuals and companies. But this common notion is a myth. The free market does not create monopolies; governments create monopolies by granting one organization the exclusive privilege of doing business or by establishing *de facto* monopolies through regulatory agencies whose alleged purpose is to ensure competition but whose real effect is to limit it.

Why Socialism Cannot Work

No doubt about it: for many intellectuals, socialism has snob appeal! It is chic to be a socialist! According to Paul Hollander,

> The appeals and values associated with socialism . . . have provided the most powerful incentive for the suspension of critical thinking among large contingents of Western intellectuals. . . . Such intellectuals appear to assume an affirming, supportive stance as soon as a political system (or movement) makes an insistent enough claim to its socialist character. . . . The word "socialism" has retained, despite all historical disappointments associated with regimes calling themselves socialist, a certain magic which rarely fails to disarm or charm these intellectuals and which inspires renewed hope that its most recent incarnation will be *the* authentic one, or at least more authentic than previous ones had been.[8]

Of course, Hollander continues, "there is little evidence that intellectuals, or for that matter nonintellectuals, living in countries considered Socialist are similarly charmed or disarmed by the idea of socialism."[9]

The miserable performance of socialist economies is no accident. There is a fundamental reason why socialist economies do not work: *they cannot.* Austrian economist Ludwig von Mises developed the argument that supports this contention in

8. Paul Hollander, *Political Pilgrims: Travels of Western Intellectuals to the Soviet Union, China, and Cuba* (New York: Oxford University Press, 1981), 416, 417.

9. Ibid., 417.

1920.[10] According to Mises, socialism can never work because it makes economic calculation impossible. And because it makes economic calculation impossible, socialism makes rational economic activity impossible.

One of the greatest advantages of a market system is the constant supply of information it provides through the price mechanism. A socialist system does not provide that information. Tom Bethell explains the socialist's problem this way:

> It is one thing for central planners to draw up a plan of production. It is quite another to carry it out. . . . How can you (the planner) know what should be produced, before you know what people want? And people cannot know what they want unless they first know the price of things. But prices themselves can only be established when people are permitted to own things and to exchange them among themselves. But people do not have these rights in centrally planned economies.[11]

Without free markets to set prices, socialists can never attune production to human wants. The impossibility of precise measures of cost accounting under socialism will result in economic disaster. Mises did not deny that rational action might still be possible under socialism with regard to small and insignificant matters. But under a system that ignores profit and loss, it would be impossible for production to be consciously economical. Rational economic production, which proceeds from rational economic calculation, would be impossible.

Most socialist countries, including the Soviet Union, kept the economic chaos at a minimum by imitating the pricing system of the free market. But the only reason socialist economies could function at all was that their bureaucratic managers carefully monitored the pricing information generated by free markets and then applied it to set their own prices. When they

10. Mises's argument was originally published in German. For an English translation, see Ludwig von Mises, *Socialism: An Economic and Sociological Analysis*, trans. B. Kahane (New Haven, Conn.: Yale University Press, 1951).

11. Tom Bethell, "Why Socialism Still Doesn't Work," *The Free Market* (November 1985): 6, 7.

ignored or could not obtain this information from free markets, their problems became even more serious.

The great paradox of socialism is that it needs capitalism in order to survive. Unless socialists make allowance for some free markets to provide the pricing information that alone can make rational economic activity possible, socialist economies must collapse. As a consequence, socialism cannot dispense with market exchanges. Socialism, then, is a gigantic fraud, a parasite that attacks the market at the same time that it uses it to survive.

One other reason for socialism's inevitable failure must be noted. A market system provides important incentives that are simply missing under socialism. Brian Griffiths explains that under socialism, "rewards are not related to effort and commercial risk-taking, but to party membership, bureaucratic status, political fiat and corruption. As a consequence, the legitimate commercial entrepreneurial spirit is killed; for perfectly understandable reasons, people devote their resources to hacking a way through the political and bureaucratic jungle of their economies."[12]

After examining the course of socialism in the Soviet Union, Eastern Europe, China, Cuba, Nicaragua, and other Third World nations, sociologist Peter Berger concluded, "Even in the early 1970s it should not have been news that socialism is not good for economic growth and also that it shows a disturbing propensity toward totalitarianism (with its customary accompaniment of terror)." Claims by the leaders of such nations that their adoption of socialism reflects their commitment to justice and equality are not simply empty rhetoric; they are hypocritical deceit. "Put simply," Berger declares, "Socialist equality is shared poverty by serfs, coupled with the monopolization of both privilege and power by a small (increasingly hereditary) aristocracy." While the world largely accepted the

12. Brian Griffiths, *The Creation of Wealth* (Downers Grove, Ill.: InterVarsity, 1985), 26.

inevitability of this elitist aristocracy in the Soviet Union, the same phenomenon showed up in every socialist state. "It seems to be the intrinsic genius of socialism to produce these modern facsimiles of feudalism."[13] He concludes: "We know, or should know, that socialism is a mirage that leads nowhere except to economic stagnation, collective poverty, and various degrees of tyranny."[14]

What should we think of church intellectuals and self-proclaimed liberation theologians who tell us that socialism is the only economic system compatible with Christianity? What does their claim tell us about their understanding of economics? What does it tell us about their moral sensitivity, to say nothing of their sensitivity to the millions who have suffered, and the millions more who will continue to suffer, from such systems?

The Moral Attack on Capitalism

Socialists have always seemed to sense that if the battle between capitalism and socialism were fought on the grounds of economic theory and practice alone, their cause was hopeless. Hence, socialists have always preferred to attack capitalism on moral grounds. Even if capitalism is superior economically, they argued, it must be curtailed or rejected on moral grounds. Let us examine two of the more popular of these moral attacks.

First, capitalism often has been attacked on the ground that it exploits poor people and poor nations. A crucial but often unstated assumption of this view is that the only way some can become rich is by exploiting others. This assumption reduces to the claim that market exchanges are examples of what is called a *zero-sum game*. In a zero-sum game, only one participant can win. If one person (or group) wins, then the other must lose. Baseball and checkers are two examples of zero-sum games. If A wins, then B must lose.

13. Peter L. Berger, "Underdevelopment Revisited," *Commentary* (July 1984): 41, 43.
14. Ibid., 45.

The error here is thinking that market exchanges are a zero-sum game. On the contrary, market exchanges illustrate a *positive-sum game*. In a positive-sum game, both players may win. We must reject the myth that economic exchanges necessarily benefit only one party at the expense of the other. In voluntary economic exchanges, both parties may leave the exchange in better economic shape than would otherwise have been the case. Both parties gain through the trade because both value what they receive more than what they give. If they did not perceive the exchange as beneficial, they would not continue to take part in it. Once again, free market exchanges exemplify the peaceful means of exchange: if you do something good for me, then I'll do something good for you.

Second, socialists criticize capitalism for encouraging greed. However, the market mechanism actually neutralizes greed by forcing individuals to find ways to serve those with whom they wish to exchange. Undoubtedly, market exchanges often bring us into contact with greedy people. But so long as our rights are protected (a basic condition of market exchanges), their greed cannot harm us. As long as greedy individuals are prohibited from introducing force, fraud, and theft into the exchange, their greed must be channeled into the discovery of products or services for which we are willing to trade. Every person in a market economy has to be other directed. Participation in the market requires concern for others. Far from pandering to greed, the market tightly restricts greed by prohibiting its satisfaction except by service to others. Thus it allows natural human desires to be satisfied only in a nonviolent way. The alternative to the peaceful means of exchange is coercion.

But there is plenty of reason to fear greedy people in socialist and interventionist systems. There they need not serve others to get what they want in free exchanges. They need only bribe politicians to give them privileged positions in the economy (something interventionists achieve through such innocent-looking mechanisms as licensure and regulation) or to take for them what they want by force of law (something socialists do through the innocent-sounding mechanism of redistribution).

Morality and the Market System

Many enemies of capitalism fail to appreciate that capitalism can be defended on grounds not only of its economic superiority but also of its moral superiority to socialism.

Help for the masses. Critics of capitalism fail to see how much the market process improves the lot of the masses. It is impossible to ease, reduce, or eliminate poverty by constantly dividing the economic pie into smaller pieces. There simply is not enough wealth to go around then. Poor people don't need continually smaller pieces of a shrinking pie. They don't need to argue over how the economic pie should be divided. They need a bigger pie.

Liberation theologians are convinced that capitalism offers no hope to the Third World. But the evidence is clear, Michael Novak argues, that "those third world countries that follow the capitalist model soon join the ranks of 'developed' nations, e.g., the capitalist nations of East Asia."[15] Liberationists need to pay more attention to the dramatic ways in which socialist countries have been forced to adopt capitalist measures. As Novak points out, "Socialism was not invented as a system designed to produce economic development. Its main historical purpose has been political control. The socialist ideal of economic organization is rapidly being modified by a thousand capitalist qualifications because of repeated historical failures in the one sphere [socialism] and success stories in the other [capitalism]."[16]

The last thing Latin America needs is a socialist revolution that will only produce more of the state control that causes so many of its present problems. The only hope for Latin America's poor is a genuinely capitalist revolution, a revolution that successfully avoids the damaging state controls of interventionism.

15. Michael Novak, *Will It Liberate? Questions about Liberation Theology* (Mahwah, N.J.: Paulist, 1986), 46.
16. Ibid.

Third World countries that adopt a market economy grow more rapidly than those that insist on governmental planning and control of the economy. The amazing economic performance of Hong Kong and other Southeast Asian nations like Taiwan, South Korea, and Thailand demonstrates how a government can encourage economic growth by following a market approach.

It may seem that all we have done in this section is simply to return to the theme of capitalism's indisputable economic superiority. Not really. If providing genuine economic relief for the poor is a moral endeavor, then capitalism's practical success and socialism's practical failure have obvious *moral* implications: they demonstrate the moral superiority of capitalism over socialism.

Political freedom.   Political freedom is a vitally important human value. But economic freedom is a necessary condition for personal and political liberty. No one who lacks economic freedom can be free in the political sense. Economic freedom enhances political liberty by limiting the concentration of too much power in the hands of too few people. As long as a large percentage of the people in a society exercise ownership control, power within that society will be widely diffused. But no one can be free when he depends wholly on others for his basic economic needs. If someone commands what you can or cannot buy and sell, then a significant part of your freedom has been abridged. People dependent on any one power for the basic essentials of life are not free. When the state becomes master, obedience becomes a prerequisite to employment and to life itself. Leon Trotsky put the point sharply: "In a country where the sole employer is the State, opposition means death by slow starvation. The old principle: who does not work shall not eat, has been replaced by a new one: who does not obey shall not eat."[17]

17. Cited in Friedrich A. Hayek, *The Road to Serfdom* (Chicago: University of Chicago Press, 1944), 119.

Because economic collectivism destroys political and spiritual freedom, economics is the front line in the battle for freedom. While capitalism is not a *sufficient* condition for political freedom in the sense that it *guarantees* it, the difficulty of finding nations with significant political freedom that do not provide for economic freedom indicates that capitalism is very nearly a *necessary* condition for political freedom.

Private ownership and moral behavior. More attention needs to be given to the important ways in which private ownership stimulates the development of moral behavior. British economist Arthur Shenfield once wrote,

> Every time we treat property with diligence and care, we learn a lesson in morality. . . . The reason for the moral training of private property is that it induces at least some of its owners to treat it as a trust, even if only for their children or children's children; and those who so treat it tend to be best at accumulating it, contrary to popular notions about the conspicuous consumption of the rich, the incidence of luck or of gambling. Contrast our attitudes to private property with our treatment of public property. Every army quartermaster, every state school administrator, every bureaucratic office controller, knows with what carelessness and lack of diligence most of us deal with it. This applies everywhere, but especially in socialist countries where most property is public.[18]

Shenfield is right. People do treat their own property differently than public property or the property of others. This fact can teach people some important moral lessons.

Everything has a cost. Once we realize that few things in life are free, that most things carry a price tag, and that therefore we will have to work for most of the things we want, we can learn a vital truth about life. Capitalism helps teach us this

---

18. Arthur Shenfield, "Capitalism Under the Tests of Ethics," *Imprimis* (December 1981).

truth. But, Shenfield warns, under socialism, "Everything still has a cost, but everyone is tempted, even urged, to behave as if there is no cost or as if the cost will be borne by somebody else. This is one of the most corrosive effects of collectivism on the moral character of people."[19]

The result of the moral test. Many religious critics of capitalism focus on what they take to be its moral shortcomings. In truth, the moral objections to capitalism turn out to be a sorry collection of arguments that reflect, more than anything else, serious confusions about the true nature of a market system. When capitalism is put to the moral test, it more than holds its own against its competition. After all, it makes little sense to reject one system on moral grounds when all of the alternatives turn out, in the real world, to have far more serious problems. To quote Shenfield again, among all of our economic options, only capitalism

> operates on the basis of respect for free, independent, responsible persons. All other systems in varying degrees treat men as less than this. Socialist systems above all treat men as pawns to be moved about by the authorities, or as children to be given what the rulers decide is good for them, or as serfs or slaves. The rulers begin by boasting about their compassion, which in any case is fraudulent, but after a time they drop this pretense which they find unnecessary for the maintenance of power. In all things they act on the presumption that they know best. Therefore they and their systems are morally stunted. Only the free system, the much assailed capitalism, is morally mature.[20]

The alternative to free exchange is coercion and violence. True, capitalism allows natural human desires to be satisfied, but only in a nonviolent way. Little can be done to prevent human beings from wanting to be rich. But capitalism channels that desire into peaceful means that benefit many besides those

19. Ibid.
20. Ibid.

who wish to improve their own situation. "The alternative to serving other men's wants is seizing power of them, as it always has been. Hence it is not surprising that wherever the enemies of capitalism have prevailed, the result has been not only the debasement of consumption standards for the masses but also their reduction to serfdom by the new privileged class of Socialist rulers."[21]

Capitalism is quite simply the most moral system, the most effective system, and the most equitable system of economic exchange. When capitalism, the system of free economic exchange, is described fairly, there can be no question that it comes closer than socialism or interventionism to matching the demands of the biblical ethic.

Michael Novak's Theology of Creation

Today, any adequate evaluation of capitalism and socialism must take into account a new twist to the subject that Novak began to develop in the mid-1980s. In his 1986 book *Will It Liberate?* Novak argued that it is time to replace so-called theologies of liberation with what he calls a *theology of creation*. He began by referring once more to the lessons taught by the astounding economic gains of the nations of Southeast Asia:

Consider the nations of the East Asia Rim (notably South Korea, Taiwan, Singapore, Hong Kong, but also Japan and others). At the end of World War II these nations were among the poorest, most devastated and seemingly resourceless nations on the planet. Within twenty-five years, they had multiplied their national wealth many times over, raised up most of their poor, and become economic leaders of the world. By 1985, their standard of living was coming to rival that of Southern Europe. In the next fifteen years, some predict, their standard of living will be higher than that of Northern Europe.[22]

21. Ibid.
22. Novak, *Will It Liberate?* 76.

This economic miracle can teach us several things. For one, it is still possible for significant economic development to occur within a relatively short time. For another, economic growth does not depend on access to natural resources. "If natural resources were the cause of the wealth of nations," Novak writes, "Japan and other nations of the East Asia Rim would be poor; their natural resources are few. The cause of wealth is the human wit and human discipline through which peoples organize themselves for communal, associative *creativity*."[23] The ultimate sources of wealth are human intelligence and discipline, which in turn lead to activity, cooperation, and invention. "Human wit creates employment through inventing goods and services never seen before. . . . everything we today call a 'resource' was invented by human wit. Until human wit works on them, the givens of nature have no use. Economic value comes from human creativity."[24]

This is why Novak is more interested in talking about *creation theology* than *liberation theology*. He insists that creation theology is also interested in liberating people from political tyranny and poverty. But the proper way to achieve this liberation is not revolution, not the destruction that preoccupied the older, radical liberationists. The best means to true and lasting liberation is creation. He explains: "First to be created are institutions that encourage human beings to act as true images of God: to become creative in a routine and regular way. For creativity is a social achievement. It must be achieved by a whole society acting together. It is not the fruit of one person alone. Without a supportive society, even the greatest genius is frustrated. A whole society must be organized to favor creativity."[25]

Novak's words here are directed against the leaders and institutions of poor nations that prevent human creativity from being loosed. More often than not, poverty within a nation is fostered by the stupidity or corruption or both of heavy-handed leaders of the state, whose stupidity and corruption are more

23. Ibid., 77.
24. Ibid.
25. Ibid.

deadly under socialism because socialism encourages the concentration of economic and political power.

> [A] crucial condition for genuine liberation is that no one group of men, arrayed with a panoply of all the coercive powers of the state, gain all power over politics, over economics, and over morals and culture. The absorption of all of life by politics, and of politics by the state, is the Achilles' heel of existing socialist regimes. The separation of systems, the separation of powers in short, the hard-won lessons of liberal societies do in fact achieve such splendid liberations as humanity has ever yet achieved.[26]

This last paragraph reveals the essential link between Novak's theology of creation and his claim that the North has had its own liberation theology for two centuries. The combination of a free-market economy and limited constitutional government is the most effective means yet devised to impede the concentration of economic and political power in the hands of a small number of people. Every person's ultimate protection against coercion is his having control over some private sphere where he can be free. Private ownership of property is an important buffer against any exorbitant consolidation of power in government. Political institutions like constitutional guarantees of freedom of speech and separation of powers do more than preserve liberty; they also help provide an environment that encourages human creativity.

One would never learn from the writings of liberation theologians that democracy is growing in Latin America. Yet according to Novak, "Ninety percent of the population of Latin America now lives again under the beginnings of democratic government."[27] But democracy is only one side of the coin. "Part of the promise of political economy is not only to liberate human beings from arbitrary tyranny, but also to liberate human beings from poverty. Political economy has two sides: democracy and economic growth."[28]

26. Ibid., 31.
27. Ibid., 78.
28. Ibid.

Novak is not simply saying that it would be nice if the developing democracies of Latin America could also begin to grow economically. "The success of democracy, in fact, depends on economic growth. A democracy must create new wealth that did not exist before, new wealth for all to share. Democracy must be creative, or it will come to be rejected (much to the loss of its citizens). Above all, democracy must liberate the creative energies of its people."[29]

It is impractical to pursue the details of Novak's creation theology any further except to say that he rejects the view that a nation's wealth trickles down in various ways from the top. Rather, wealth "wells up from millions of small entrepreneurs at the base in, so to speak, base communities. . . . A nation in search of creativity must, therefore, empower millions of small associations at its base. Wealth wells up from the inventiveness, activism, and creativity of millions of small producers and entrepreneurs."[30] Political liberation (freedom from tyranny) and economic liberation (freedom from poverty) require a nation to do everything possible to allow each citizen to become what Novak calls an economic activist. The state must eliminate obstacles that prevent or hinder people from starting businesses. Tax laws should encourage creativity, not punish it.

A final qualification is necessary to head off the inevitable cries from the Left. Novak wants it understood that his theology of creation is not about *laissez-faire*:

It is not about free enterprise alone. On the contrary, commerce and industry can blossom only where law and a common universal morality are observed. As their source lies in the human spirit, so they must obey the laws of the human spirit, or they will perish. Democracy depends on the rule of law. All must abide by that law. But, in addition, economic activities can prosper only under a system of reliable and well-respected law, and only where the moral law is obeyed. For economic activities in

29. Ibid., 78–79.
30. Ibid., 80–81.

a free society are free, voluntary, mutual. They depend on the
free cooperation of many, on trust swiftly arrived at, and on
mutual reliability. The more lawlike and moral a people, the less
costly its economic life. Every human vice and failing injures
sound economic activity.[31]

Novak's call for creation, for capitalism, for economic freedom does not entail a radical individualism, a dog-eat-dog selfishness. Creativity and economic growth require cooperation
and community.

While Latin America desperately needs change, the writings
of the radical liberation theologians give us no hope that the
realization of their dreams will produce liberation from either
tyranny or poverty. Like other regions that have produced their
own versions of liberation theology, what Latin America needs
is a new liberation theology, a true liberation theology that will
learn from the much older liberation theology of the North that
economic growth is possible and that the creation of wealth is
necessary if economic liberation is ever to become a reality. But
this new liberation theology will also be what Novak calls a
theology of creation in which governments get out of the way
and allow human intelligence and drive to produce economic
activity in a moral and spiritual environment that encourages
true community. Both the gospel and a faithful, witnessing,
serving church have a necessary role to play in this task.

Some have dared to suggest that the vision and goals of creation theology approximate the objectives of many who see
themselves as liberation thinkers. If liberationists ever begin to
recognize that the best means of achieving their goals includes
not socialism but democratic capitalism, we may finally have
reason to hope for the future of Latin America and other
regions of the Third World. Then what has been a liberation
theology in name will finally begin to bear fruit in genuine liberation from both tyranny and poverty.

31. Ibid., 81–82.

5

Liberation Theology and the Bible

The older liberation theologians' claim to represent a *Christian* perspective on things invites an analysis and evaluation of how loyal they have been to the historic Christian faith. They get in trouble from the start by surrendering in an embarrassingly uncritical way to a host of post-Enlightenment presuppositions that leave them with a Scripture that cannot function normatively or authoritatively. They compound their problems by subjecting the Bible to their problematic hermeneutic, or method of interpretation. In all their approach to Christian belief, as in their social analysis, they are captive to the Left-wing mind-set of the day.

Some Background Information

At the close of the twentieth century, the major challenge confronting the Christian faith is the crisis of unbelief spreading rapidly in the church. Such unbelief, of course, is hardly new. Christianity has always had those within its gates who have used Christian language, symbols, and institutions but have altered the essence of the faith. Pretending to be Christianity's

115

prophets, priests, and gatekeepers, they have subverted the faith, creating a totally different religion more acceptable to their tastes. When honesty meant more than civility, they were called heretics and were asked to peddle their new creeds outside the city walls. But a major change began around the middle of the nineteenth century.

Until then, Roman Catholics and Protestants shared a common belief that this world is the creation of a personal, almighty God whose providence displayed itself in history. They also agreed about the general historical reliability of the Gospels in reporting the teachings and miracles of Jesus. They agreed that Jesus' death was a sacrifice for human sin that was followed by his miraculous resurrection from the dead. This Catholic-Protestant consensus (otherwise known as orthodoxy) dominated Christian thought well into the nineteenth century.

But a century and a half ago, a process began that was to remove Christian orthodoxy from its central place as the unifying force in Western life and culture. Doctrinal nonconformists and heretics, who formerly would have left the church or been expelled, began to teach their views *within* the church. Unbelief began unrelentingly to take up residence in the church. The Catholic-Protestant consensus on essentials like the Trinity, the deity of Christ, the incarnation, the resurrection, Jesus' death as a sacrifice for human sin, the human need for redemption—all these were attacked not only by people outside Christianity, who had always rejected them, but increasingly by individuals who now insisted on being denominational leaders or seminary professors. This anti-supernatural, anti-revelational, anti-Trinitarian, and frequently anti-theistic new religion dominated much of American and European Protestantism for the first half of the twentieth century.

Richard John Neuhaus describes the kind of unbelief that passes for theology in present-day Catholic and Protestant liberalism:

The new class of the diffuse denomination that is Catholic-Protestant Liberalism is . . . supremely confident about the implausibility of what millions of Americans believe. "A Christian in the modern world can no longer believe such and such," they authoritatively declare. But of course there are all kinds of Christians in the modern world who believe precisely such and such. The new class ploy in response to this embarrassing reality is that such Christians are simply stupid. Or, if such Christians are indisputably very smart, it is said that they are living in the nineteenth century.[1]

The new class of liberals that pretends to speak for contemporary Catholicism and Protestantism is not interested in reaffirming the historic Christian faith. As Neuhaus explains,

> Between reaffirming the faith and reconceptualizing the faith, reconceptualizing wins hands down. It is the very stuff of the academic and publishing industries. If there were no need for thorough reconceptualizations, fundamental reexaminations, moral transvaluations, hermeneutical revolutions, and historic-ocritical transformations, there would be no need for all the people who are very expensively trained to engage in just such things. Those who resist the efforts of such talented people are perceived to be anti-intellectual because most of the people who are paid to be intellectuals are on the other side.[2]

In chapter 1 we noted the devastating effect of radical biblical criticism on Latin American Protestants like Rubem Alves. Their loss of confidence in the Bible weakened their commitment to historic Christian beliefs, and they became ready targets for the totally new understanding of Christianity that became the basis of their radical liberationism. As we noticed, some of those radicalized Protestants now no longer regard themselves as Christians, even in the most extended sense of the word.

In the rest of this chapter, we will examine several elements of the liberal view of the Bible that appears with great frequency

1. Richard John Neuhaus, *The Catholic Moment* (San Francisco: Harper and Row, 1987), 81–82.
2. Ibid., 79.

in liberationist writings. We will notice that these views cannot help but lead to truncated and even heretical views of Christian belief. We will also see how groundless these critical views of Scripture are. Liberation theologians have traded their Christian birthright for a mess of liberal pottage.

One place to find the views under consideration is the writings of Leonardo Boff, who states: "One cannot always decide in a convincing manner whether or not a particular saying did or did not come from Jesus, even though in the present elaboration in the Gospels it is uttered by Christ. Form criticism permeates this entire study [i.e., Boff's book]."[3] Boff readily admits his skepticism about the authenticity of many sayings attributed to Jesus.[4]

While Boff exemplifies the influence of form criticism, Jon Sobrino operates under the influence of redaction criticism when he writes that biblical claims about Jesus' titles and major events "already embody a later process of theologizing in the Jesus event. Chronologically they come after Jesus himself, introducing us to an already developed Christology."[5] Sobrino believes that much of the New Testament teaching about Jesus grows out of later reflection of Christians who lived, most likely, between 75 and 85 A.D. He doubts the historicity of many well-known gospel events, such as Jesus' birth in Bethlehem, Herod's command to kill the children, the visit of the wise men, and so on. Even more serious is his skepticism about the portrait of Jesus presented in the New Testament.

According to Phillip Berryman, the New Testament Gospels "give access to Jesus only through the eyes of Christian communities several decades after his life." Students of the New Testament will recognize immediately that Berryman's claim is grounded on assumptions associated with form criticism. This means, for example, that the "Sermon on the Mount is not a

3. Leonardo Boff, *Jesus Christ Liberator: A Critical Christology for our Times,* trans. Patrick Hughes (Maryknoll, N.Y.: Orbis, 1978), 34.

4. Ibid.

5. Jon Sobrino, *Christology at the Crossroads: A Latin American Approach,* trans. John Drury (Maryknoll, N.Y.: Orbis, 1978), 5.

verbatim record of Jesus but a collection of sayings attributed to him." This claim is typical of religious liberals who have accepted a particular approach to the New Testament. Berryman is convinced that almost everything the New Testament says about Jesus' deeds and words is up for grabs. He is a liberation theologian who believes the only healthy approach to the alleged historicity of the Gospel accounts is skepticism. In the next sentence, he reveals his elitist scorn for the Catholic scholarship of earlier generations: "Only in the last twenty-five years has Catholicism fully accepted the results of modern biblical scholarship."[6]

In order to see how much is wrong in Berryman's approach to the Bible, an approach replicated by almost all of the old liberation theologians, it will be necessary to take a brief detour into contemporary biblical criticism, specifically to understand the influential methodologies of form criticism and redaction criticism. The old liberation theologians' uncritical appeal to these and other problematic methodologies should not pass unchallenged. Nothing in these methods entailed the skeptical conclusions liberationists drew in concert with hard-core liberal Protestants and Catholics.

Form Criticism

According to form criticism, the Gospels are not simply historical narratives about Jesus. They are the end result of a long process of oral tradition that was collected, preserved, and edited.[7] Primitive Christianity first passed on its memories and traditions about Jesus' life and teaching orally. Gradually this became a kind of oral tradition that assumed different forms (pronouncement stories, miracle stories, paradigms, and so on). As time passed, some of these sayings were lost. But others came to be valued for their practical importance in solving

6. All three quotes from Berryman appear in his *Liberation Theology* (Philadelphia: Temple University Press, 1987), 61.

7. Radical form critics believed that the church not only preserved and passed on the tradition about Jesus but actually created or reshaped it.

problems that began to develop in the church. As form critics saw it, the traditions about Jesus that survived did so because a particular life situation (*Sitz im Leben*) in the early church provided a reason for their preservation. For example, the story of Jesus picking grain for food on the sabbath supposedly was preserved because of its relevance for a problem within the early church about sabbath observance.

Form critics viewed the Gospels as the product of a long and complex process by which an original collection of oral traditions came to be preserved because of their practical relevance for the church at a time much later than eyewitness testimony. They emphasized the role of the Gospels as interpretations of Jesus' life and teaching. They de-emphasized the earlier search for objective, dispassionate eyewitness reports about what Jesus did and taught. For the form critic, then, the Gospels were an important source of information about *what the church believed about Jesus at the time the Gospels were formulated*. The extent to which the Gospels were also reliable sources of information about the historical Jesus became a question to which form critics gave different, often conflicting answers.

Several positive contributions of form criticism stand out. For one thing, its stress on a period of oral tradition prior to the writing of the Gospels countered an earlier emphasis on exclusively written sources for the Gospels and sought to move beyond the problems inherent in that approach. It also drew important attention to the fact that the community of the early church had a practical interest in the tradition it transmitted. Form criticism helped clarify how the practical concerns of the early Christian community shaped and preserved its memories of Jesus. Form critics correctly noted that the Gospels were written for specific reasons. The selection and arrangement of material in the Gospels reflected practical concerns addressed by the writers.

It is important to distinguish between the *neutral method* of form criticism, which can be useful in a number of ways for understanding Scripture, and the *presuppositions* that some form critics insist on bringing to their use of the method. Like most neutral methods, form criticism can be used for destructive purposes when controlled by negative presuppositions. Form critics who became captive to these destructive presuppositions used their method to undermine the historical credibility of the Gospels. Consequently it became difficult to get behind the Gospel material to find the real Jesus. This same skepticism about the historical Jesus prevails among certain liberation thinkers.

By itself form criticism does not force one to conclude that the early church *invented* its stories about Jesus. The method can be used by people who believe the stories were recollections of what Jesus actually did and said, recollections that were preserved because of their relevance for some later life situation in the church. Historian A. N. Sherwin-White comments, "It is astonishing that while Graeco-Roman historians have been growing in confidence, the twentieth-century study of the Gospel narratives, starting from no less promising material, has taken so gloomy a turn in the development of form-criticism that the more advanced exponents of it apparently maintain . . . that the historical Christ is unknowable and the history of his mission cannot be written."[8]

The problem then is not with form criticism per se but with the undefended assumption that the Gospels witness primarily to the life situation of the church at some later stage of its history and only secondarily to the historical Jesus. But surely it is consistent with the form critical method to recognize both the role that a later life situation might have had in preserving a tradition and the reality of the historical events to which the tradition points. Instead of assuming that the early church fabricated stories about Jesus to help it deal with its problems, it makes better sense to assume that considerations about practical relevance led the church to preserve statements originally made by Jesus. D. M. Baillie, for one, complained that it sel-

---

8. A. N. Sherwin-White, *Roman Society and Roman Law in the New Testament* (New York: Oxford University Press, 1963), 187.

dom seemed to occur to some form critics "that the story may have been handed on simply or primarily *because it was true*, because the incident had actually taken place in the ministry of Jesus, and was therefore of great interest to his followers, even if they sometimes failed to understand it."[9]

The kind of skeptical form criticism that has been used to undermine the reliability of historical statements about Jesus in the Gospels can be attacked on several grounds. First, the position depends on the questionable assumption that the early church had little interest in the actual deeds and sayings of Jesus. Second, the skeptics assume that the Gospels are primarily preaching documents that are unconcerned with either biography or history. Certainly the Gospels were not written as biographies of Jesus. Nor were they merely historical accounts free of any theological interest and perspective. But it is surely an overstatement to claim that the Gospels show no concern with biographical or historical truth.

Another questionable assumption of much contemporary historical skepticism is that the historical reliability of a Gospel is necessarily suspect if the Gospel has a theological motive. The historical skeptics never tell us why an interest in theological matters is necessarily incompatible with an interest in historical truth or (if we grant them their assumption for the sake of argument) why their own interest in theological matters is not incompatible with an interest in historical truth!

It is one thing to note that the Gospel writers selected from the material available to them and applied it to practical uses. It is quite another to suggest that they felt no constraints against inventing new traditions if doing so suited some practical purpose. While the biblical writers obviously felt free to select and adapt their material, they worked under an obligation to preserve the truth about what Jesus actually did and taught. Selectivity does not entail creativity. Theological concern does not necessarily imply disdain for historical accuracy.

9. D. M. Baillie, *God Was in Christ* (New York: Scribners, 1948), 57.

In an important article in the *Anglican Theological Review*, theologian William G. Doty drew attention to several other criticisms of the form critical method. He pointed out that skeptical form critics fail to "take seriously enough the possibility that Jesus consciously formulated his sayings with the intention of securing them for transmission."[10] After all, any good teacher wants to assure that what he teaches will be remembered and transmitted accurately. Moreover, Doty continued, skeptical form critics play down the important role of eyewitness testimony to what Jesus said and did:

> Critics who have been dismayed by the form critics' negative historical evaluations have stoutly defended the historicity of the synoptic materials by reference to the probability that the traditions were secured for the early communities by eyewitnesses. These critics [of form criticism] point to the possibility that first generation Christians were either still living, or had carefully passed on their first-hand experiences to the compilers of the gospels.[11]

Other critics have faulted skeptical form criticism for its almost exclusive preoccupation with the life situation of Christianity *after* the resurrection of Jesus. But why exclude the life situation of Christians involved in the public ministry of Jesus as a possible influence on the tradition? Why should a form critic restrict himself to considering life situations *after* Easter? Skeptical form critics adopt an arbitrary starting point for their method when they hesitate to look earlier than the end of Jesus' earthly life and consider that there might have been life situations *before* Easter that could have given rise to and affected the transmission of the traditions.

A pivotal issue in the debate concerns proper placement of the burden of proof. The skeptics argue that the burden of proof rests on those who regard the sources as authentic. But as

---

10. William G. Doty, "The Discipline and Literature of New Testament Form Criticism," *Anglican Theological Review* 51 (1969): 304. Doty's article is on 257–319.

11. Ibid., 304.

New Testament authority Joachim Jeremias asks, "Why should the burden of proof not fall on the skeptic?"[12] Why not presume that if anything is to be proved, it must be the *in*authenticity of some saying of Jesus? Catholic scholar Neil McEleney points out how Jeremias's presumption accords more closely with accepted journalistic practice:

> This debate over the "burden of proof" points up the importance of the criterion which I shall call "historical presumption".
> . . . Briefly, it is this, that one accepts a statement upon the word of the reporter unless he has reason not to do so. In other words, in the normal course of human affairs, one does not suspend judgment when told that a certain speaker has said something but presumes competence and reliability upon the part of the reporter and accepts his word unless there are reasonable grounds for denying it. Without such presumption, all histories, news reports, etc., are open to rejection, and we can have no assurance of what we do not immediately experience. This presumption, then, tips the balance in favor of the authenticity of words attributed to Jesus where no reason makes us suspect otherwise. Of course, one can be mistaken or be deceived in accepting the word of a reporter and only discover the truth later on, but this does not affect the basic principle that the presumption is in favor of veracity, and where this means assertion of authenticity, it is in favor of authenticity.[13]

Jeremias explains, "We are justified in drawing up the following principle of method: In the synoptic tradition it is the inauthenticity, and not the authenticity, of the sayings of Jesus that must be demonstrated."[14] The eagerness with which almost all of the old liberation theologians embraced skepticism about the historical information in the Gospels hardly recommends them as students of the Bible or interpreters of the Christian tradition for the poor of Latin America.

12. Joachim Jeremias, *New Testament Theology* (London: SCM, 1971), 37.
13. Neil J. McEleney, "Authenticating Criteria and Mark 7, 1–23," *Catholic Biblical Quarterly* 34 (1972): 446–47.
14. Jeremias, *New Testament Theology*, 37.

Redaction Criticism

Another method common in the writings of old liberation theologians is redaction criticism. While form critics concentrate on smaller independent units of material within the Gospels, redaction critics are more interested in the Gospels as literary wholes. Instead of viewing the Gospel writers as people who simply collected and passed on material, redaction critics acknowledge the role of the Evangelists as theological interpreters of the tradition. They see the Gospel writers as more than "scissors-and-paste men" who merely isolated blocks of material and arranged them. They were more than mere compilers and arrangers; they were theological writers whose arrangement of material was affected by both their theological interests and their intention.

But why should any of this lead anyone to assume that the Gospel writers *invented* material? It needn't. As easy as it may be to notice theological interests at work in the Gospels, it requires a whole set of additional presuppositions to conclude that the Evangelists produced only imaginative interpretations of Jesus with loose or even nonexistent historical ties. As Stephen S. Smalley points out, the radical claim that there is no connection between the Christ of faith and the Jesus of history presupposes

> that the evangelists themselves were unaware of the distinction between history and faith, and were prepared to disregard the former completely in the interests of the latter. We are not, in fact, compelled to believe that this was the case. If the Gospel writers were, on the contrary, sensitive to what was historical and what was kerygmatic (as there are real grounds for supposing), it is unlikely that they would have treated their traditional sources for the words and works of Jesus with anything but respect. All the more would respect have been shown by the evangelists, indeed, if (as is probable) eyewitnesses were still around.[15]

15. Stephen S. Smalley, "Redaction Criticism," in *New Testament Interpretation*, ed. I. Howard Marshall (Grand Rapids: Eerdmans, 1977), 188–89.

In other words, redaction criticism and form criticism are not necessarily incompatible with either a high view of Scripture or the conviction that the New Testament picture of Jesus is grounded on historical information. Conservative use of redaction criticism suggests that the Evangelists started with the historical information available to them and "drew out the theological implications of history which they recorded."[16] Starting with the apostolic tradition about Jesus, the Evangelists expressed their own theological understanding of the tradition by the arrangement of their Gospels and by the seams that tied the various units of tradition to one another.

Used with care, redaction criticism provides students of the New Testament with several advantages. It can help them see the interrelationship between faith and history in the early Christian community. The Gospel writers were not interested in recording *bare* facts. The Gospels reflect their writers' interaction with and theological interpretation of history. Redaction criticism also stresses the importance of studying the Gospels as wholes and not as loose compilations of smaller independent units. Redaction criticism can help identify what the Gospel writers themselves contributed to their source material. It can also unveil the major reasons each Evangelist had for writing his interpretation of the traditions.

But many redaction critics perform highly conjectural and subjective analysis. Redaction criticism should not imply the creation of new material. Redactional activity by the Evangelists does not force a choice between history and faith, between the apostolic tradition and the theological interpretation of the Evangelists.

The historical skepticism about the deeds and sayings of Jesus that appears so frequently in the writings of the old liberation theologians raises serious questions about their competence in both biblical studies and logic.

16. Ibid., 189.

The Denial of Revealed Truth

Liberation theologians' writings reveal more than the influence of a liberal critical methodology. They show the presence of another tenet of liberal thought: the denial that God can reveal propositional truth to people.

This assumption appears in the writings of José Míguez-Bonino, who undoubtedly picked it up during his studies in liberal North American seminaries. According to Míguez-Bonino, the Word of God should not be understood "as a conceptual communication but as a creative event, a history-making pronouncement. Its truth does not consist in some correspondence to any idea but in its efficacy to carrying out God's promise or fulfilling his judgment."[17] Theologically liberal Protestants realized that they could make Christian communities much more pliable to their imaginative, subjective reconstructions of Christian belief if they could dissuade the people in the pew from the old idea that divine revelation was in any sense "conceptual communication." Interpret the Word of God in any way you like, as inward personal experience or as "creative event" perhaps, but never as a communication of truth! Over the past two hundred years, much non-orthodox theology has tried to deny Christians any access to divinely revealed truth. Since God has not spoken and, indeed, cannot speak, the human relationship to God must be understood according to some model other than that of receiving information or truth.

The rejection of the possibility of revealed truth achieved the status of an official doctrine in many Protestant and Catholic circles. British thinker John Hick summarized the view:

Revelation is not a divine promulgation of propositions, nor is faith a believing of such propositions. The theological propositions formulated on the basis of revelation have a secondary status. They do not constitute the content of God's self-revelation but are human and therefore fallible verbalizations, constructed

17. José Míguez-Bonino, *Doing Theology in a Revolutionary Situation* (Philadelphia: Fortress, 1975), 89–90.

to aid both the integration of our religious experience into our own minds and the communication of religious experience to others.[18]

This position amounts to the claim that humans can never attain knowledge of whatever God might want them to know. Whatever else religion can and possibly should be, it can never be grounded on revealed information from God.

The consequences of this are far reaching. For one thing, it explains the tendency in so much contemporary Christendom to equate the Christian religion with whatever "Christians" happen to believe or practice at the moment. Since there is no divinely revealed truth, we may believe whatever we want. In practice, the religion professors who propagate this view want our freedom limited to believing whatever *they* happen to be *saying* at the moment.

But where, we might ask, are the arguments necessary to support this distinctively modern claim? There are none. The theory has gained wide acceptance simply because it has become part of the theological mind-set in many departments of religion, a mind-set, incidentally, that can easily be traced back to Friedrich Schleiermacher in the nineteenth century and Immanuel Kant in the eighteenth. Moreover, the doctrine of revealed truth that is so widely rejected today ends up being a straw man, while the most serious problems with the new, noncognitive view of revelation are simply ignored.[19]

Other Troubling Signs

It is disconcerting to see those who function as religious leaders simply following the lead of earlier blind leaders. When we investigate how these religious leaders got from point A to point B, we discover that later individuals simply parroted what earlier people said. At no point in the process between A and B

18. John Hick, *Faith and Knowledge*, 2d ed. (Ithaca, N.Y.: Cornell University Press, 1966), 30.

19. For an expansion and defense of the points in this paragraph, see Ronald H. Nash, *The Word of God and the Mind of Man* (Grand Rapids: Zondervan, 1982).

do we ever encounter anything that might remotely be considered an *argument*. But as groundless as the ideas we have noticed in this chapter may be, they certainly have consequences. And the consequences of the uncritical assumption of views that undermine the authority of divine special revelation inevitably include a rejection of essential Christian beliefs.

One rather surprising source for such views is Catholic priest and philosopher Arthur McGovern, who states, "What we accepted for centuries as *the* Christian message often showed itself, under investigation, to be a very historically conditioned, interpretation." As if to support this claim, he refers to what he calls Leonardo Boff's "striking insight that much of our Christian interpretation of salvation resulted, in great measure, from the personal problems of St. Paul, Augustine, and Luther."[20] Where, one is led to inquire, is the "striking insight" in all this? Perhaps Father McGovern has not studied much Protestant theology since Schleiermacher; anyone who has will recognize immediately that Boff's claim is derived from familiar liberal Protestant efforts to recast all of Christianity's historic teachings in its own humanistic image, the target in this case being the New Testament's teaching about human sinfulness and justification by faith.

Of course, we cannot rule out the possibility of one difference between Boff's rejection of New Testament soteriology and that of the old Protestant modernists. The liberal Protestants tended to reject all talk about human sin in favor of a belief in the inherent goodness of each human person. Boff's rejection of the inspired Pauline teaching about salvation may stem from his opposition to viewing sin as a corruption of the individual person. It fits liberationist thinking better to see sin as a feature of the structures of society. This is the most likely reason why Berryman doesn't take the Genesis account of the fall of man seriously. While he tolerates some treatment of sin as individual failure, what interests him more is a view of sin as

20. Arthur F. McGovern, *Liberation Theology and Its Critics: Towards an Assessment* (Maryknoll, N.Y.: Orbis, 1989), 158. The allusion to Boff concerns material in the latter's *Liberating Grace*, trans. John Drury (Maryknoll, N.Y.: Orbis, 1979), 23.

something affecting social structures. This accords more closely with his collectivist social instincts.[21]

Orthodox Christians have no difficulty understanding how individual sin comes to have a structural character. But they are obviously dissatisfied with any view of sin that fails to see it as an offense to a holy God and a violation of God's holy law. When sin as transgression is denied or de-emphasized, it is impossible to do justice to a biblical understanding of Christ's redemptive work and the salvation grounded on it. When one sees the work of liberationists in this context, he can hardly be surprised to find some of them equating salvation or the kingdom of God with the process of liberation as they define it.[22]

Berryman seems noticeably uncomfortable in the presence of the historic Christian understanding of Jesus' death as a sacrifice for human sin.[23] He prefers seeing Jesus as a martyr to his "subversive message." He is also vague about the resurrection of Jesus: "Whatever the 'historical'[24] core of the resurrection narratives, they signal God's vindication of Jesus' life and message," which he understood in the political way that we have come to associate with him.[25]

After reading Berryman for a while, it seems natural to see him as someone thoroughly controlled by naturalistic presuppositions. Such presuppositions lead people to believe that miracles are impossible, a view that certainly seems to underlie his account of the feeding of the five thousand:

> Jesus' miracles are viewed not primarily as proof of a divine origin but as signs. Jesus' feeding of five thousand people with a few loaves and fishes is taken as a sign of the messianic banquet. Did Jesus indeed "multiply" loaves and fishes? A generation ago

21. See Berryman, *Liberation Theology*, 48.
22. See Leonardo Boff and Clodovis Boff, *Salvation and Liberation* (Maryknoll, N.Y.: Orbis, 1984), 116.
23. See Berryman, *Liberation Theology*, 56.
24. It is natural to wonder why Berryman thinks it so important to place the word *historical* in quotes. Apparently he doesn't rate the historicity of the Gospel narratives very highly.
25. Berryman, *Liberation Theology*, 48.

the emphasis was on the divine power manifest in such ability to "suspend" the laws of nature. Scholarship today[26] shows that the authors themselves were most intent to see the occasion as a sign of the promised messianic banquet present already inchoatively in Jesus. Hence, to see this account as expressing Jesus' solidarity with the poor and as a sign of the kingdom is closer to the original sense than to take it as part of a rationalistically constructed chain of reasoning moving from Jesus' power and authority to his "founding" of a church, and the transmission of that authority to the present church through the pope and bishops.[27]

Basic to naturalism is the unprovable assumption that the natural order is self-sufficient and self-explanatory. The miraculous content of biblical Christianity is rejected not because it cannot be defended against this or that philosophic or scientific claim but because it is logically incompatible with the religious commitment many moderns have made to a naturalistic worldview.[28] Once this leap of faith to naturalism is made, everything else in the liberal's view of things is as easy as sliding down an icy hill.

Hermeneutics

The faulty logic that we have already noticed in liberationist appeals to form and redaction criticism is also apparent in liberationism's peculiar hermeneutic. *Hermeneutics* is a term usually used to refer to the science of interpreting written texts, especially the biblical text. Liberation theologians early in their history developed their own peculiar way of interpreting the Bible. The Bible must be understood, they claimed, from the perspective of the poor. The historical situation of the poor and the necessary praxis required to attack the causes of poverty must function as the lens through which the Bible is read. They

26. Note the question-begging appeal to modernity as presumed authority.

27. Berryman, *Liberation Theology,* 61.

28. Naturalism as a worldview suffers a devastating critique at the hands of C. S. Lewis in *Miracles: A Preliminary Study* (New York: Macmillan, 1963).

are *the* important factors in determining the meaning of the biblical text. According to Berryman, people in base communities "understand the Bible in terms of their experience and reinterpret that experience in terms of biblical symbols. . . . Interpretation moves from experience to text to experience."[29] As an example he cites John 12:24, which quotes Jesus speaking about a grain of wheat falling and then dying. While the original application may have been to Jesus' death, the poor in base communities might well apply it to the death of some martyred leader.

Berryman writes as if no one in seminary ever pointed out to him the rather obvious difference between the *one meaning* of a text and the *many applications* it might have for people in different circumstances. Religious teachers for centuries have edified their students by allegorizing or spiritualizing biblical passages. But no one with any theological training or respect for the Bible would ever confuse this type of application with discerning the primary sense of the text. We would hate to think that the liberationist mission rests very heavily on such an obvious oversight.

But there are other troubling aspects of the liberationist hermeneutic. When older liberationists were criticized for approaching the biblical text so subjectively, they were prone to respond that they were only doing what everyone does. All of us, they argued, read the Bible through our own grids, which include highly personal, cultural, and class elements.

This claim must not go unchallenged. It is true that our understanding of many things is colored, influenced, and occasionally even biased by perspectival considerations.[30] For example, every human being has a worldview, often held unconsciously, that exercises an enormous influence over everything he thinks. A dedicated proponent of the Christian worldview will, of necessity, understand what the New Testament says about Jesus Christ differently than a Muslim, humanist, or New Age devotee. But the most foolish and self-

29. Berryman, *Liberation Theology*, 60.

30. See Ronald H. Nash, *Faith and Reason* (Grand Rapids: Zondervan, 1988), chaps. 1–4.

defeating thing any liberationist could say is that *all* of these contexts, perspectives, or worldviews are equally good. Once the liberationist assents to such hard-core relativism, he has forfeited any claim to a respectable hearing for his own interpretation. He has reduced himself to saying that while *you* might have *your* interpretation, *he* has *his*.[31] In a world in which all interpretations are equally good or true, all interpretations are also equally bad or false! The credibility of liberation theology depends on the liberationist's being able to assert that his understanding of things is *true, period*. If all he can say is that his view is true *for him*, there is no reason for anyone to take his claim seriously.

Not all interpretations, then, are born equal. The real challenge of hermeneutics is to identify an approach to the biblical text that will enhance our chances of understanding its primary sense. The approach that does this best is well known to students of the Bible. It is the *grammatico-historical method*. All this means is that we do our best to understand the meaning of the author's language and set his words in their proper historical and textual context. While hermeneutics is hardly an exact science, the number of truly pivotal passages with serious interpretive problems is surprisingly small. But all that is necessary to refute the self-defeating position of hermeneutical relativism[32] is one biblical text the meaning of which is indisputable. We have such texts in abundance. For those who demand an example, we offer the shortest verse in the Bible: "Jesus wept" (John 11:35).

So what is the most that any reasonable liberationist hermeneutic can possibly supply? The answer is that it can encourage the poor to read the Bible and see how certain texts may *apply* to them in a spiritual or allegorical sense. A responsible liberationist interpreter of Scripture will also point out carefully in

31. See Ronald H. Nash, *Christian Faith and Historical Understanding* (Richardson, Tex.: Probe, 1984), chap. 5.

32. Hermeneutical relativism is self-defeating because if it were true, no one with a different hermeneutic would ever be able to determine the meaning of the hermeneutical relativist's (including the liberationist's) own writings.

such cases what the primary sense of the text is. Once the poor are encouraged to study the Bible, they will, of course, find many passages that refer directly to them and their situation. But the time has come to put away all the nonsense about liberation theology having a unique hermeneutic. To the extent that it is new and unique, it gives false readings of Scripture. To the extent that it gives correct readings of the Bible, there is nothing new or unique about it.

In previous chapters, we have noticed that the liberationists' understanding of economics, social philosophy, and even Marxism is seriously flawed. In this chapter, we have examined equally serious problems with their approach to and understanding of the Bible. Given their liberal, culture-bound approach to the Bible, it would probably take a miracle for them to arrive at an understanding of Christian doctrine consistent with historic Christian orthodoxy. Unfortunately, this is one time when many liberationists seem able to draw a logical inference. The result is highly subjective deviations from historic Christian teaching.

Any true liberation theology must be able to offer human beings liberation from sin. To do this, the representatives of that theology must have a correct biblical understanding of the nature of human sin and God's divinely given remedy for sin in Jesus Christ. But before we can hope to see a genuinely Christian presentation of the atonement and resurrection, we are going to have to see signs of a more responsible and faithful approach to God's inspired and authoritative Word.

6

Liberation Theology and Social Theory

The debate over liberation theology has helped spark a renewed interest in the study of Latin American societies. As new insights (for example, those in Hernando de Soto's *The Other Path*)[1] force observers to examine hitherto unexplored issues, old assumptions about Latin America's poverty, history, and problems are challenged. Many efforts at understanding the intricacies of the region's problems should be welcome responses to liberation theology's call to study the causes of poverty scientifically.

Beyond Dependency Theory

As we have seen, one of liberation theology's battle cries has been that truly effective love for the poor demands an effort to understand the roots of poverty; only then will we know how to liberate the poor from its yoke. As Gustavo Gutiérrez has put it,

1. Hernando de Soto, *The Other Path: The Invisible Revolution in the Third World*, trans. June Abbott (New York: Harper and Row, 1989). Mario Vargas Llosa wrote the preface.

"Lyrical but vague statements in defense of the dignity of the human person are completely ineffective insofar as they do not take account of the causative factors underlying the existing social order. . . . a scientific line of reasoning is absolutely necessary." This view was endorsed by the Vatican's 1984 *Instruction on the Theology of Liberation*, which said, "It is clear that scientific knowledge of the situation . . . is a presupposition for any plan capable of attaining the ends proposed. It is also a proof of the seriousness of the effort."

In the two decades between the mid-sixties and the mid-eighties, the founders of liberation theology believed that the major cause of Latin America's underdevelopment and poverty was the structures of "capitalist dependency." They diagnosed most of Latin America's ills from poverty to instability as by-products of capitalist domination and of the alleged dependence of the region's economies on the needs and interests of the developed (i.e., imperialist) nations. To cure the disease, liberationists usually prescribed radical revolution and socialism. Understandably, their weak sociological analysis came under increasing fire from many quarters, especially during the eighties.

Three major sociological criticisms to liberation theology appeared. First, some objected that its practitioners failed to live up to their own commitment to scientific methodology. Such a commitment should have implied a readiness to explore a multiplicity of causes and to subject all hypotheses to empirical testing. Critics pointed out that liberationists utterly failed to provide evidence for their theses. Liberationists wrote as if their conclusions were *a priori* assumptions, valid for all circumstances and beyond any need for empirical verification.

Second, liberationists were accused of reducing most causes of the dismal state of Latin Americans to a single sociopolitical cause (dependency) while failing to pay serious attention to the influence of other cultural or institutional elements. Especially poignant in this regard was the charge that they were indulging in the old and pernicious Latin American practice of blaming others and failing to look critically at themselves. Jean François

Revel had in fact made the caustic remark that "Latin American civilization may be the first ever to avoid self-criticism entirely."

Third, liberationists were faulted for what seemed a simplistic tendency to prescribe socialism as a redemptive or liberating sociopolitical system while neglecting to specify the type(s) of socialism they endorsed. They remained totally silent about why they believed their sociological and economic prescriptions were superior. These and other criticisms were articulated in both the religious and the social science communities.

Some of the earliest criticisms of liberation theology came from the Vatican. Among its objections was the claim that, in liberationist analyses, "The ideological principles come prior to the study of the social reality and are presupposed in it." Even authors like Dennis McCann, whose sympathy with the humanitarian goals of liberationists is well known, found regrettable the liberationists' uncritical endorsement of dependency theory. He also criticized their lack of scientific scrutiny of other answers.

The empirical flaws of liberationist social analysis were first exposed in the early seventies in a celebrated essay by Argentinean sociologist José Luis de Imaz.[2] Decrying the lack of conceptual precision in terms like *dependent*, Imaz demonstrated the lack of correlation between degrees of dependency (however defined) and underdevelopment. The same conclusion was corroborated by many other researchers, who to their shock, as Lawrence E. Harrison puts it, found "that there is a correlation between the degree of dependency, as measured by trade and capital data, on the one hand, and income inequality and political participation, on the other." But the correlation goes "strongly and significantly in the opposite direction from that predicted by dependency theory." Countries that, according to economic indicators, rank high in dependency (like Canada) also exhibit far higher degrees of development than coun-

2. See José Luis de Imaz, *Los Que Mandan* (*Those Who Rule*), trans. Carlos Astiz (New York: State University of New York Press, 1970).

tries like Haiti, whose economies are less entwined with those of the "imperialist" nations.

The explanatory weakness of dependency theory brought a new set of diagnoses of what was wrong with Latin America's societies. Two studies worth mentioning in this regard were those by Chilean Joseph Ramos, for whom the fundamental problem is not dependence or economic growth, but economic distribution,[3] and Michael Novak, for whom the cause of Latin America's disgrace was not capitalism but the region's failure to develop its variant of mercantile capitalism into full-blown democratic capitalism.[4]

An important contribution of Novak is to shift attention from the causes of poverty to the causes of wealth. Following the lead of Adam Smith, he stresses the essential role of enterprise. He sees enterprise as a locus of creativity and initiative as well as a catalyst in producing wealth, new goods, and services. Paraphrasing Friedrich Hayek's observation that under capitalism, silk stockings previously available only to the duchess became available to working-class women, he described capitalism as a key element in lowering costs and making previously scarce goods more readily available. Capitalism also creates new markets, jobs, and savings. And it contributes educationally by teaching people the value of taking into account the needs and preferences of consumers, employees, and the public at large. A system that discourages enterprise, Novak suggests, necessarily discourages its fruits as well.

By the mid-eighties, scholars had reached a growing consensus about the complexity of the problem of poverty and development and the need to move in a truly undogmatic, scientific fashion. If the plight of the poor were to be understood, it was necessary to be more serious and careful in studying their social conditions. The dismal economic performance of Eastern Bloc economies helped produce widespread disillusionment with

3. See Ramos's chapters in *Liberation South, Liberation North*, ed. Michael Novak (Washington, D.C.: American Enterprise Institute, 1981).

4. See Michael Novak's *The Spirit of Democratic Capitalism* (New York: Simon and Schuster, 1982).

socialism and undermine earlier confidence in the virtues of collectivist solutions. Even Gutiérrez argues, in a recent book, for a critical approach to the analyses of poverty by the social sciences. He maintains that they should be subjected to continual evaluation and revision.[5]

By the close of the eighties, it had become clearer that what remained of liberation theology was not so much its sociology as its call to take up the cause of the oppressed. This, in turn, requires a serious commitment to understanding the social roots of the region's sufferings.

If positions like the one raised in de Soto's *The Other Path* have sparked so much interest, it is because they have challenged old assumptions while heightening awareness about the richer complexity of causes at work in Latin American societies. As we shall soon see, these new insights can provide a rich and relatively uncharted course to those committed to reflecting theologically on the issues of oppression and liberation.

The Two Peruvians

It may be an irony that Peru, the birthplace of liberation theology's founding father, is also the homeland of the two men who have done the most to redefine the terms of the discussion about liberation from oppression: Hernando de Soto and Mario Vargas Llosa. Unlike a host of theologians, authors, and academics who still dominate the region's intellectual life, these new Peruvians do not blame outside malevolent forces for the chronic ills that affect their societies. Quite the opposite. They denounce this tendency as an obsession that looks like "Freudian transference." This transfer of guilt to others may be comforting to many Latin Americans, argues Vargas Llosa, but it may well be one of the greatest obstacles in the task of overcoming underdevelopment. As long as their countries fail to recognize that "the principal cause of their crisis resides in them-

5. Gustavo Gutiérrez, *We Drink from Our Own Wells: The Spiritual Journey of a People*, trans. Matthew J. O'Connell (Maryknoll, N.Y.: Orbis, 1984).

selves, in their governments, in their myths and customs, in their economic culture . . . the evil will not be rooted out."

Vargas Llosa and de Soto have made a conscientious effort to break with this pattern by looking to the inner workings of Latin American societies. What they have found may help to free liberationist thinking from some of its past bondage to ideological presuppositions.

What keeps the region in chronic poverty, they claim, is the statism typical of the "centralist tradition." Originally coined by Chilean sociologist Claudio Veliz,[6] the term refers to an old Latin American trait that leads people to "expect all from one single person, institution, myth, powerful and superior ruler, before whom everybody abdicates his civil responsibility."

The centralist tradition has led to the growth of giant and powerful states and state bureaucracies at the expense of individual initiative. Those social monsters are highly interventionist, arbitrary, inefficient, and corrupt. They not only suck out wealth and resources from society, but also, through their suffocating controls and red tape, actively discourage, if not prevent, the creative and productive entrepreneurship of private citizens. The implicit organizing principle of these governmental bureaucracies is to redistribute income rather than generate it. Such systems cripple the economy and corrupt society. According to de Soto, "A legal system whose sole purpose is redistribution thus benefits neither rich nor poor, but only those best organized to establish close ties with the people in power. It ensures that the businesses that remain in the market are those which are most efficient politically, not economically."[7]

An added consequence of these systems is a politicizing of all sectors of the population. Each group battles to secure for itself protection or advantages from the state. "Consumers press for prices below competitive levels, wage earners press for wages above them, established business people try to prevent or delay

6. Claudio Veliz, *The Centralist Tradition of Latin America* (Princeton, N.J.: Princeton University Press, 1980).

7. de Soto, *The Other Path*, 191.

any innovation that might damage their position, and employ-ees exert pressure to keep their jobs and avoid replacement by more efficient workers," de Soto argues.[8]

The Peruvians contend that belief in a strong (read "big") interventionist state as a means to promote development and social justice runs very deep among elites at both ends of the ideological spectrum. All too often, intellectual and religious elites characterize private business in terms of selfishness and greed; such enterprises supposedly have no purpose other than the production of unjust profits for their owners. They envision social (state) ownership, however, as more altruistic, sensible, and progressive. Regulations, taxes, and all sorts of controls are thus seen as means to ensure that the social good is served by those who otherwise would impose their greed on the popula-tion. The Peruvians concur with P. T. Bauer's statement that Third World elites have bought wholesale the socialist illusion about the intrinsic goodness of all state action and that there-fore they tend to view sympathetically most of the enlargements of the power and attributes of the state.

For Vargas Llosa, these biases are wrongheaded and have produced catastrophic results. How does one explain, he asks, why a country like Argentina, which fifty years ago was one of the most developed nations of the world, now has one of the world's most chaotic and precarious economies? How does one explain why Venezuela, one of the most fortunate nations on earth, is incapable, after decades of an oil-generated bonanza, of securing its future, and why it now shares the insecurities and upheavals of other poor Latin American nations? How does one explain why Peru, which thirty years ago was the number one producer of fish flour and, for a time, the number one fishing nation in the world, now finds these industries ruined and sub-sidized? The answer is always the same: statism. In all those cases, the state became a giant that confiscated or overregu-lated key industries: it harassed private initiative, it fixed prices,

8. Ibid., 192.

it granted privileges, and it ruled over the economy in an arbitrary, heavy-handed fashion.

By punishing entrepreneurship, the new Peruvians argue, the centralist tradition hinders the growth of creativity, wealth, and development. The end results of its policies are thus poverty and economic stagnation. The "misery villages" or belts of poverty that surround Latin American cities are populated not by victims of capitalism or American imperialism but by victims of a mercantilist, redistributivist, centralist tradition.

As de Soto found out, the Latin American poor try to escape the grip of these evils with inventiveness and resourcefulness. One of their avenues of escape is the creation of the informal sector (what Vargas Llosa calls "capitalism of the poor"), which is that vast underground economy where the poor set up their own businesses outside the existing legal framework. There a true market economy works, albeit harassed and limited by the constraints of the formal, state-sanctioned one.

Beyond Peru

Although de Soto never claimed that his book describes what he found anywhere but in his native Peru, evidence is mounting that his diagnosis applies to most of Latin America. Since its publication, de Soto has received numerous letters and messages from people in nations like Mexico, Ecuador, Argentina, Venezuela, and Colombia reporting that his descriptions of Peru fit perfectly things they have observed in their homelands.

Research along the same lines as de Soto's has produced similar results. In Mexico, for instance, Oscar Vera Ferrer has provided fresh evidence about the asphyxiating red tape that the poor must cope with in pursuit of their most elementary aims. When a group of peasant farmers (*campesinos*) of the State of Sonora petitioned for title to a tract of undeveloped land, they waited for two years to receive a terse letter from a federal bureaucrat saying the petition was denied because of lack of corroborating documentation, notwithstanding the thirty-five

pages of details they had prepared with the help of local law-
yers.

Sandinista Nicaragua provides additional witness to the ago-
nizing struggle between many of the "informals" and the impla-
cable encroachment of the state. Especially pathetic has been
the case of the street vendors and the merchants of Nicaragua's
formerly thriving informal markets. The Sandinista government began by demanding that they obtain registration
licenses. Then it set up strict limits on the amount of goods
merchants could store, on the alleged grounds that there was a
need to fight "hoarding" and "speculation." Then it set up quo-
tas fixing the amount of products they could buy every month.
Next it decreed prices and went into a frenzy of harassing,
arresting, or driving out of business vendors accused of not
complying with the state ordinances. The battle cry of these
poor Nicaraguans, drawn not from any ideological predisposi-
tion but from their simple need to survive, became "Freedom
of Commerce!" (There were also many instances of agricul-
tural workers petitioning the state to return confiscated farms
to their former employers.)

It would be a mistake to assume that the informals make up
only a minority of Latin America's poor. In fact, the urban
informals and the peasants who are also small entrepreneurs
account for more than half of Latin America's economically
active population. In countries like Nicaragua, Peru, and Mexico, informals far outnumber the classical proletariat (urban,
propertyless workers, hired by mid- to large-sized industries).
Most Latin American poor are small, informal entrepreneurs.
When they are not, as may be the case with some "purer" pro-
letarians, they often marry, support, or co-habit with small,
informal entrepreneurs.

A New Patch for a Theology of Liberation: Liberation from Oligarchic and Bureaucratic Power

For these vast masses of productive, resourceful, yet crushed
people, there has not yet been a theology of liberation that artic-

ulates their concerns. There are hopeful new signs, however, as in the case of the writings of the Peruvians and a new breed of Latin American authors. Another promising sign is the recent papal encyclical *Sollicitudo Rei Socialis.*

In this document, John Paul II defends the "Right of Economic Initiative." Denying this right, the pope says, "destroys the spirit of initiative." In its place, he continues, "there appears passivity, dependence, and submission to the bureaucratic apparatus which, as the only 'ordering' and 'decision-making' body . . . puts everyone in a position of almost absolute dependence." The pope sees this right in the dignity of the human person. Whoever denies it oppresses the individual and creates a need for liberation.

A new theology of liberation would then heed the call to advocate liberation from coercive institutions, private or public, that stifle the lives and entrepreneurship of the poor while further impoverishing them and society. Novak's words in regard to the duties of teachers of Catholic social thought fully apply here:

> They should criticize statist practices and customs that block the flowering of creative talents in economic enterprise, that keep markets open solely to established firms and existing monopolies and blocked to all others; that make legal incorporation a lengthy, expensive and corrupt procedure; that fail to establish institutions that supply credit to the poor, humble, or relatively unknown persons. . . . Teachers of Catholic social thought should make certain that the ways of enterprise are open especially to the poor.

Dependency theory may also be recast and given new impetus. Scholars may explore in more depth the role that *dependency on the state* has had in perpetuating poverty. A theology of liberation recast in the spirit of the right of economic initiative would have a distaste for bureaucratic central planning and would favor the maximum expansion in society of independent, autonomous economic units.

One merit of this approach is that it distances itself from both monopoly capitalism and statism. In fact, from this new perspective, monopoly capitalist and socialist regimes (both of which, as we saw in chapter 4, are statist) are all part of a continuum. Both are enemies of private property, for they concentrate it either in the hands of a few private individuals or in the hands of the state. Both are enemies of individual initiative, for they rule the economy through the decisions of small, privileged elites, either private oligarchs or upper-rank bureaucrats.

The new perspective calls for the democratization or multiplication of property against its private or public concentration. If there should be protection for any, let it be protection for the entrepreneurship of the poor. This type of sociopolitical thinking sides with the common person. Yet it does not necessarily advocate extreme individualism. Citizens can unite or pool their resources in small or large endeavors, cooperatives, joint enterprises, or communal settlements according to their wishes and cultural traditions. Policies sensitive to the latter would make sure that the right to economic initiative of such autonomous collective units would be respected.

Basing a theology of liberation on these different approaches would entail a reassessment of terms like *revolution, progressive,* and *reactionary.* A true, progressive revolution, or set of policies, takes place whenever the autonomy and power of the poor (as independent social, moral, and economic units) increases. Any regime, Left or Right, that makes the poor subservient to bureaucratic or oligarchic power is reactionary.

The Voice of the Poor

The contentions of the new breed of Latin American writers become even more challenging to traditional liberationist thinking in the area of who speaks for the poor.

Being able to express the views of the poor or, as they put it, becoming the "voice of the voiceless" has been a theme dear to liberation thinkers. Liberationists have consistently claimed that their views offer just a theological articulation of pleas of the Latin American poor. In fact, Gutiérrez introduced one of his earliest essays on this theme by saying that the "other side, of the poor and the exploited, has begun to make his voice heard, and in their struggle, they demand that private owner-ship of the means of production will be eliminated because it enables the few to expropriate the fruits of labor performed by the many. . . ."

But according to Vargas Llosa, the poor peasants and urban dwellers alike are crying out *for* private ownership and free enterprise. He illustrates this point in telling of his recent trip to the fishing village of Atico, in southern Peru, at the request of its humble and impoverished fishermen. What did they want? "That the only industry of the place, a fish flour factory, be privatized." He explains,

> Those who out of a sharp instinct know what the problem is and how to cure it at its roots, those who mobilize themselves and fight to liberate those industries from the dictatorship of the state in order to return them to civil society, those are not the politicians, not even the entrepreneurs, some of whom of a ren-tier mentality see with distrust a privatization that would bring to the market new competitors. . . . Those are the poor, the fish-ermen, their wives and their children.

State ownership and its corresponding central planning may be far closer to the hearts of European or North American uni-versity professors than to the hearts of the vast majority of Latin America's poor. Statistically speaking, advocates of public own-ership are represented more among the academic establish-ment than among working-class communities. Recent research, like that by Michael Radu and others, corroborates that revolu-tionary ideas of the kind expressed by Gutiérrez and others invariably come from the privileged, even aristocratic classes who seek the support of alienated Western people to pursue their own elitist agenda.

The very existence of the informals challenges the socially concerned Christian with the need to articulate his pledge before the power centers of society. The latter include not only the state and its functionaries but also the intellectual, religious, academic, and better-positioned elites. Among these, one of the greatest obstacles for providing the informals with a receptive hearing is ideological prejudice which often disguises its subtle forms of cultural or racial prejudice with a veneer of paternalism.

Listening to the voice of the voiceless can indeed be humbling for elites trained in the conviction of their own intellectual superiority. It is important not only to know what the poor say they want, which is a simple though neglected empirical question, but also to be ready to admit that what they want may often be best for them. They have, as Vargas Llosa and the pope have said, a sharp instinct born not so much out of academic training as out of experience. The person who wears the shoes knows better where they hurt than the designer. John Paul II perceived the "evangelical instinct" of the humble and simple faithful in regard to how they "spontaneously sense when the Gospel is being served . . . and when it is being eviscerated and asphyxiated by other interests." Not only in economics but also in other issues, it seems that the poor know best.

This reflection should not be read, however, as a blanket endorsement of anything that the poor may wish. The voice of the majority, or the oppressed, is not epistemologically privileged. The truth of any proposition should be judged on its own merits, not on the merits of its proponents. What we are suggesting is that liberation theology will more truly reflect the wishes and yearnings of the poor when it ceases attributing to them an ideology of statism that they abhor and begins listening more carefully to their instincts. In doing so, Christian activists may discover that the masses of slum dwellers, peasants, street vendors, shoppers, and humble people of Latin America are clamoring for liberation from coercive statist controls. They may learn that the poor are indeed demanding their right to chart their own course, the right of economic initiative. In this regard, the actions of the informals, more than their words, may be a better expression of their need.

We began this chapter by noting how poorly the outdated appeal to dependency theory by all of the old liberation theologians now fares in the world of the 1990s. We then explored aspects of the important work of the two Peruvians, de Soto and Vargas Llosa. Although the insights and findings of the Peruvians are invaluable, they are confined to what we might call institutional or sociostructural analysis. Their approach provides a novel and needed diagnosis of *one* cause of poverty in Latin America, for which they offer institutional remedies. But de Soto and Vargas Llosa do not address other, specifically cultural, causes that play extremely important roles in the perpetuation of poverty and social ills. In the following chapter, we will examine the cultural dimension in some detail.

7

Liberation Theology and the Culture of Poverty

In the last chapter, we expressed our appreciation for the pioneering work of Hernando de Soto and Mario Vargas Llosa. As valuable, however, as is their analysis of how the institutional structures of Latin American nations make escape from poverty so difficult, nonetheless they ignore ways in which assorted moral and cultural considerations compound the problems of the poor in the South.

The Peruvians are not necessarily at fault for this omission, which could be attributed to the specialized nature of their research or to the need to emphasize a vital but neglected aspect of Latin American societies. The error would be to make the "centralist tradition" *the* all-encompassing, sufficient cause for the social and economic ills of Latin America. Such a view would be as flawed as the earlier reductionism of liberation theology, except that it would replace dependency theory with the centralist tradition.

The search for a comprehensive explanation of the social ills afflicting Latin America still requires a careful consideration of the role played by other factors, especially moral and cultural elements. I (the writer is Humberto Belli) was sensitized to the significance of these aspects firsthand when, in 1974, as a young sociologist with some radical ideas, I visited the fishing community of Puerto Morazan, in the northern coastal provinces of my country of birth, Nicaragua. The purpose of my visit was to investigate the villagers' failure to develop successful economic cooperatives.

The local shrimpers could have benefitted enormously from using motor-propelled boats instead of the traditional paddle-canoes, from co-owning and co-managing a sizeable commercial freezer, and from using a decent fleet of vehicles to market their products. The money and the know-how to set up this project were made available by the government and a private foundation. In return, the villagers were expected to run their cooperative enterprise. But the project ran aground. One after another of the cooperative's treasurers stole the money; drivers used the vehicles for personal gain, often selling the new tires and parts; the shrimpers neglected the freezer's maintenance until it broke down. Furthermore, the several fishermen who made a relatively high surplus spent it at the nearby bars and brothels to the silent dismay of their wives or common-law companions.

Although the villagers could be classified as informal, in this particular case it was clear that they were not victimized by a noxious set of regulations or similar bureaucratic, legal, or economic constraints. In fact, they were protected informals and could enjoy their right to economic initiative almost to their hearts' content. The sources of their failure lay elsewhere.

As I still analyze this case, it strikes me as obvious that their problem lay in their values (or lack of them), their weak moral standards, and the breakdown of their families. Their problem was rooted in culture, not in socioeconomic structures.

The village's inhabitants needed to be educated in the broadest sense of the word. They needed a grounding in morality, at least in regard to stealing and in habits of discipline, thrift, and responsibility. But how could they learn these things when their families were failing to perform the minimal function of socialization?

Families in Puerto Morazan were in disarray. Male (father) absenteeism was rampant. Mothers, abandoned to their own resources and overburdened by financial need, had to look for work themselves and send their children to work in the fields. There was little time, opportunity, or energy left for supervising or instructing the children, or for otherwise ensuring that they grew up to be responsible adults. Boys lacked good adult male models; girls resented their fathers and pitied their mothers. The miseducation of the villagers started very young and left deep scars. No amount of social engineering, government incentives, or visiting social workers could hope to rechart their lives and teach them what they had not learned when they were younger and so more teachable.

I concluded that only the rankest ideologue could believe that the collectivization of the Nicaraguan economy, or similar governmental policies, could solve these kinds of problems. For one thing, they could not make men like those at Puerto Morazan better fathers. Clearly enough, these cases called for an approach that goes beyond seeing the world exclusively in terms of social institutions or structures and attends to the important world of values, moral standards, and spiritual conditions.

The Sociology of Institutional Remedies

Surprisingly, perhaps, noninstitutional approaches to the study of Latin American societies are rare. In fact, one of the intellectual biases of our epoch is disdain for the spiritual dimensions of human life, including the roles of morals, culture, and the family in shaping society. The disdain may be open, as among classical Marxists, for whom such elements are determined by the class structure of society. But it may also be subtle, as in the widespread tendency of social scientists, historians, and journalists to overlook these factors in their analyses of social problems.

Social literature on Latin America sometimes mentions, usually in passing, such cultural aspects as machismo, family disruption, alcoholism, corruption, and the like. But these phenomena are almost invariably seen as by-products of the system. When an academic interest does develop in these areas, it is usually with the intent to show how they are rooted in the workings of the capitalist system. Such was the case, for instance, with the early Oscar Lewis,[1] who coined the term *culture of poverty*, and with Erich Fromm, who conducted in-depth analysis of Mexican peasants.

Authors of less radical leanings do not blame capitalism for the cultural pathologies they may detect, but they do tend to assume that some of these problems will gradually disappear with the advent of "modernization," usually a euphemism for capitalist development and secularization. The advocates of these views are usually future-oriented evolutionists. Most draw their inspiration from the structural-function school of the 1950s and 1960s. Although many are more sensitive to the role played by the moral-cultural dimension (they may recognize the need for an integrated moral structure) and to the importance of values like personal achievement, their emphasis still is institutional. They define problems mostly in terms of lack of economic development and place heavy reliance on state action to bring about technological development, industrialization, and more rational procedures in law and administration, secular education, and urbanization.

This kind of ideological thinking has penetrated large segments of the Christian intelligentsia including its nonradicalized members. When confronted with a society in crisis, like Latin America, today's Christian activists may search for the policies that went wrong, for the patterns of trade or land ownership that arrested development, for a better role for the state, mining, or technology. But regardless of how sound such concerns may be, few even among Christian sociologists now

---

1. See Oscar Lewis, *Five Families: Mexican Case Studies in the Culture of Poverty* (New York: Basic, 1959) and *Life in a Mexican Village: Tepoztlan Restudied* (Champaign: University of Illinois Press, 1963).

attempt to engage in what was a most normal exercise for traditional Christianity: to trace the social and historical drama to its spiritual and moral roots.

The institutional-structural bias is evident in a wealth of Roman Catholic Church documents that pay much attention to so-called structural factors but little to moral-cultural elements. When the Latin American Catholic bishops first met in Medellin in 1968, they referred in passing to the crisis in values and the critical state of the Latin American family. But they specifically claimed, "The principal guilt for the economic dependence of our countries rests with powers inspired by uncontrolled desire for gain, which leads to economic dictatorship and the 'international imperialism of money.'" Most Christians greeted the statement as a denouncement of specific sociopolitical structures thought to be the main cause of the region's problems. Although this statement could be read as an indictment of greed, which is a moral condition, it tended to assign the blame to forces outside the hearts and minds of Latin American men and women.

That so many Christians have let themselves be so influenced by the sociology of institutional remedies is perhaps one of the greatest ironies of our time, for in so doing they neglect not only a very important intellectual and scientific legacy but also key insights supplied by their own religious tradition.

Modern Scholarship and the Role of Culture

In fact, the roles of moral-cultural elements in the genesis of a vast array of social pathologies have already been the concern of respected social scientists. It is possible that much of the contemporary emphasis on the role of specific sociopolitical systems may pay too little attention to their valuable contributions. From the seminal work of Emile Durkheim on anomie[2] (a con-

2. See Emile Durkheim, *Moral Education* (New York: Free, 1961) and On *Morality and Society*, ed. Robert N. Bellah (Chicago: University of Chicago Press, 1973). See also Robert N. Bellah, ed., *Emile Durkheim on Morality and Society* (Chicago: University of Chicago Press, 1975).

dition of relative normlessness in a society or group) to the efforts of more contemporary authors like Talcott Parsons,[3] one of the overriding concerns of sociology has been the analysis of the cultural components of society. The discipline owes to scholars like Max Weber[4] and Pitirim A. Sorokin[5] the rediscovery of values as the stuff of social analysis. Values held in common, asserts Parsons, "constitute the primary reference point for the analysis of a social system as an empirical unity."

Weber's famous thesis on the role of the ethic of Protestantism in the genesis of modern capitalism has been a landmark in this regard.[6] Although it needs correction and some further elaboration, his thesis helped to establish that no responsible scholar will ignore cultural factors.

Approaches that emphasize the role of values in social life have the merit of forcing us to pay attention to the role of culture and to put in right perspective the overemphasized role of institutional arrangements. George Gilder expressed this point bluntly with regard to contemporary Japan: "The secret of Japanese [economic] success is not its industrial policy but its reactionary culture: sexist, racist and disciplinarian." In the realm of culture, we can find important clues for the success and failure of some societies.

3. See Talcott Parsons, *Action Theory and the Human Condition* (New York: Free, 1978); *Essays in Sociological Theory*, rev. ed. (New York: Free, 1964); *The Evolution of Societies*, ed. Jackson Toby (Englewood Cliffs, N.J.: Prentice-Hall, 1977); and *Social Structure and Personality* (New York: Free, 1964).

4. See Max Weber, *Basic Concepts in Sociology*, trans. H. P. Secher (Westport, Conn.: Greenwood, 1962); *Sociology of Religion*, trans. Ephraim Fischoffs (Boston: Beacon, 1964); *The Theory of Social and Economic Organization*, ed. Talcott Parsons (New York: Free, 1947); and *The Protestant Ethic and the Spirit of Capitalism*, trans. Talcott Parsons (London: George Allen and Unwin, 1930).

5. See Pitirim A. Sorokin, *Man and Society in Calamity: The Effects of War, Revolution, Famine, Pestilence upon Human Mind, Behavior, Social Organization and Cultural Life* (Westport, Conn.: Greenwood, 1968) and *Social and Cultural Dynamics* (New Brunswick, N.J.: Transaction, 1982).

6. Weber, *The Protestant Ethic and the Spirit of Capitalism*.

Values and the Economic Order

The interplay between values and economic development has been explored by several authors indebted to Weber.[7] They argue that if it is true that economic and technological conditions may affect how people think and act, it is not less true that how they think affects considerably how they handle technological and economic challenges. As P.T. Bauer insists, "Economic achievement depends on people's attributes, attitudes, motivations, mores and political arrangements." A reputable author in this field, David McClellan, conducted historical and world-scale research to provide empirical support for his thesis that levels of economic development across different societies correlate with the levels of achievement motivation found among their members.

The logic behind the work of these social scientists is simple. Any culture that considers work a curse, suited only for lesser beings, will have a harder time achieving economic development than one convinced that work is a high calling. What people believe, feel, and consider ideal has a definite and important bearing on the ways, including the economic, a society functions. As so many anthropologists, social workers, and economists can testify, deeply ingrained beliefs and behavioral patterns can be more difficult to change than institutions.

Another scholar whose vast experience in the Third World sobered his initial optimism about the possibilities of fostering economic development in backward countries was Gunnar Myrdal. After conducting massive research in India and other Asian nations, he concluded, somewhat reluctantly, that many Third World societies lack the attitudes and values that guided the rapid industrialization of the West. These societies normally exhibit low productivity, lack of responsibility on the job, poor

7. See, for example, P. T. Bauer, *Equality, the Third World, and Economic Delusion* (Cambridge: Harvard University Press, 1981) and *Reality and Rhetoric: Studies in the Economics of Development* (Cambridge: Harvard University Press, 1984); Nathan Rosenberg and L. E. Birdzell, *How the West Grew Rich: The Economic Transformation of the Industrial World* (New York: Basic, 1986); and E. Calvin Beisner, *Prosperity and Poverty: The Compassionate Use of Resources in a World of Scarcity* (Westchester, Ill.: Crossway, 1988).

compliance with standards, and lack of punctuality.[8] "All these countries demand from their people much less, and with far less results, than the Western countries."

Achievement in Latin America

What Myrdal found in Asia is what many other scholars and lay observers have found throughout most of Latin America. Its inhabitants tend to value leisure highly while they see work as something to be endured, not cherished in and of itself. Work is just the unavoidable means to make a living. Whoever works, as José Ortega y Gasset candidly admits, "does it with the more or less tenuous hope of some day gaining the liberation of his life, of reaching the hour when he will cease working to start living in the true sense of the word."

These widespread attitudes toward work with the corresponding devaluation of achievement can be discerned in the music, literature, and other folk expressions of Latin America's culture. In my youth, one of the most popular Latin hits was *El Negrito del Batey*, in which the singer celebrates that he is called the little negro of Batey, because "for me work is an enemy; I leave it to my steer since God made work as a punishment." Venezuelan Carlos Rangel notices in this regard how Hispanic Americans use expressions like "to work like a nigger" or "like a *cholo*" (Indian) to refer to excessive work. The implicit meaning of those racist expressions is that hard work is the mark of the lower classes, of the unworthy.

These attitudes seem to have early roots in Latin America's Hispanic background and in the characteristics of colonial society, in which medieval values held sway. The highest ideal of Hispanic colonial men, the *hidalgo* (man of noble origins, literally, son of somebody), scorned work, which he considered a burden to be born by lesser men or by the steer. The dream of Spanish immigrants sailing to the new continent was to become

---

8. Gunnar Myrdal, *Asian Drama: An Inquiry into the Poverty of Nations* (New York: Random House, 1972). See also his *Challenge of World Poverty: A World Poverty Program in Outline* (New York: Pantheon, 1970).

hidalgos. Saint Teresa tells that one of her brothers, in returning from "the Indies" (Hispanic America), did not want to toil on the land anymore. If in the Indies he had been a lord, would he return to Spain as a manual laborer?

There is no doubt that modernization is changing the work ethic of many Latin Americans. But Rangel observes that "only the influence of other Western countries, particularly of the United States, has been able to make a dent in the Latin American's contempt for work." Although it remains to be seen to what extent these newer influences may have drastically changed old work patterns, it is indisputable that unless the latter change, Latin America will find it harder to compete in the race with nations populated by more industrious and diligent people.

The Implications for Theology

Of course, Christians meditating on liberation cannot so easily identify economic ambition as a virtue or make rates of economic growth indicators of human liberation. The values of achievement and hard work are not exactly what Christians typically regard as the *summum bonum.* Persons may be poorer than others because they have made a choice based on the wrong priorities. Nevertheless, their understanding of work and leisure might be more consistent with Christian values than those prevalent among, say, Protestant North Americans.

Liberation theologians need to address what should be meant by a truly liberated society. Otherwise, Christians risk adopting a totally secularized ideal of liberation in which spiritual and human dimensions are sacrificed to the Moloch of material success.

Nevertheless, in meditating on the causes of poverty and other social evils, Christians and non-Christians alike need to come to terms with the empirical connection between values and rates of wealth-creating productivity. Given the proper qualifications, one could argue that in some cases there may also be a *moral* connection between some habits and some material and social consequences. As Proverbs 10:4 says, "Lazy hands make a man poor, but diligent hands bring wealth." This truth would hold even if the institutional barriers to equality of opportunity were removed.

Poverty then may result from choices that reflect significant moral and religious values. It may also result from neglect and moral weakness. Of course, it is also important not to equate economic success with the triumph of Christian virtue.

Where Christians spot laziness and lack of commitment to the duty of work, they may well speak of the need to liberate people from patterns of belief and behavior that produce oppressive results for both themselves and their descendants. In so doing, activists may broaden the understanding of liberation and make it inclusive of some personal, moral dimensions that relate to work.

Morality and the Social Order

Christians concerned with liberating people from poverty need to study how moral patterns may inhibit economic development. But they also need to give greater attention to other aspects of life not normally associated with religious concerns. These aspects include things like peace, public and private decency, order, harmonious cooperation, and fairness. A community's lack of ambition and achievement may produce lower rates of economic development, but it does not necessarily lead to a society beset by strife, crime, corruption, and similar moral maladies. A poor society may still be a decent society. The lack of some moral standards, however, destroys the very foundations of civilized life. The Bible is not the only source that spells out the connection between an individual's virtues and a proper public order, of which the economy is an integral part. Many non-Christian thinkers, from Plato and Aristotle to the present, echo the theme.

"Righteousness exalts a nation, but sin is a disgrace to any people," says Proverbs 14:34. Although the biblical understanding of greatness should not be equated with worldly greatness, since Scripture's standards are basically spiritual, the Old Testament does point out the connection between sin and observable, sociohistorical calamities, as well as between virtue and peace, order, and even material prosperity.

Sociologists could say in this regard that, although society is unique and its characteristics cannot be reduced totally to the traits of the individuals who make it up, the qualities or attributes of its individuals are decisively important to how it works. This is true whether it is a small society, like a family, or a large one, like a nation. If its members are predominantly unprincipled, selfish, or unwilling to restrain themselves, there will hardly be peace, harmony, or material prosperity. Try to imagine a working marriage under these conditions, and the truth of the proposition may become more apparent.

Individuals or societies that have not mastered the arts of self-control and rational, realistic, and moral behavior are destined for disaster. Many classical writings evidence an awareness of this and urge the importance of training citizens in virtue. Alexis de Tocqueville, in his acclaimed *Democracy in America*, observes that republican societies require a long education in liberty to prepare their citizens for the new responsibilities inherent in self-government. They call forth new virtues. In our own day, Michael Novak points to the inseparable links between vice and disorder and between virtue and good order.[9] If citizens cannot govern their own inner lives, he asks, how can they mutually govern one another in social life?

In a classic piece of anthropological research, Edward C. Banfield detected among the inhabitants of Naranjo, a rural village in Southern Italy, a trait that he terms "amoral familism."[10] This concept stands for the tendency to experience responsibility and ethical constraints only in regard to members of the same kin-group. Everyone outside that circle, including the wider community, is fair game. This trait obviously precludes the attainment of large-scale cooperation and social

9. Michael Novak, *The Spirit of Democratic Capitalism* (New York: American Enterprise Institute/Simon and Schuster, 1982), especially pp. 156–70.
10. Edward C. Banfield, *Moral Basis of a Backward Society* (New York: Free, 1958).

accountability, both vital components of the social success of groups and collectivities. Not surprisingly, the lives of the Naranjenses, while familial, were otherwise, to borrow Thomas Hobbes's phrase, "solitary, poor, nasty, brutish and short."

Myrdal found amoral familism widespread throughout most of the backward nations. In statements that complement de Soto's and Vargas Llosa's references to the centralist tradition, Myrdal said that where the market mechanisms are either non-existent or weak, "connections take their place, leading to a fragmentation of loyalties and, particularly, to little loyalty toward the larger community. From high- to low-ranking public officials, they use their power in different ways to advance their own personal ends or the interests of their families."

Social scientists have often found that in many Third World societies, the lack of drive for achievement combines with anti-communitarian moral patterns. The lack of community-oriented moral standards in public adminstration breeds corruption, which in turn hampers development and produces instability.

Corruption and Amoral Familism in Latin America

How widespread are corruption and amoral familism in Latin America? Myrdal's answer is that although a comprehensive survey of this phenomenon for this region is not available, "with individual deviations in one direction or the other, the end result has been very much the same in Latin America as in South Asia; rampant and, on the whole, increasing corruption."

Anthropologist Eric R. Wolf concurs in finding a pattern of amoral familism.[11] In Latin America, he says, "relations within the personal circle [the family] are relations of trust, of primary

11. Eric R. Wolf, *Sons of the Shaking Earth* (Chicago: University of Chicago Press, 1959). See also Eric R. Wolf, *Peasant Wars of the Twentieth Century* (New York: Harper and Row, 1970) and *Peasants* (Englewood Cliffs, N.J.: Prentice-Hall, 1966); Eric R. Wolf and Edward C. Hansen, *The Human Condition in Latin America* (New York and Oxford: Oxford University Press, 1972); and Eric R. Wolf, ed., *The Valley of Mexico: Studies in Pre-Hispanic Ecology and Society* (Albuquerque: University of New Mexico Press, 1976).

loyalty, of warmth. But relations beyond the personal circle are relations of distrust, of diminishing loyalties, of conflict both potential and actual."

Historians in fact can testify to the high degrees of anomie, corruption, and moral breakdown that have characterized the history of Latin America almost from its inception. The wars of independence that broke the bonds with Spain did not bring an end to some vicious patterns that had characterized colonial society. Instead, they often worsened them, to the despair of some of Latin America's founding fathers. Simon Bolivar, among them, was appalled by what he saw. His final judgment of the new nations, written shortly before his death, was as somber as it is telling: "I consider that, for us, [Latin] America is ungovernable. . . . The most sensible action to take in [Latin] America is to emigrate. . . . these countries [Colombia, Venezuela, and Ecuador] will ineluctably fall into the hands of a mob gone wild, later again to fall under the domination of obscure small tyrants of every color and race. . . ."

Some Latin American writers, to paraphrase Lawrence E. Harrison, are glaring exceptions to Jean François Revel's mordacious commentary about the lack of self-criticism of indigenous writers, a weakness Revel held to be a law. They have lucidly perceived moral flaws in their co-citizens. An outstanding case is Salvador Mendieta, a Nicaraguan who published *La Enfermedad de Centro America* (*The Sickness of Central America*) in 1912. To his credit, Mendieta, despite the anti-Americanism in some of his other writings, did not blame the Yankees for the misfortune of his nation. That misfortune was present before the first Yankee ever set foot on Central American soil. Instead, he attributed the region's chronic instability and underdevelopment to moral flaws like "laziness, a lack of initiative, a lack of moral courage, and an alienation from truth." Mendieta's assessment was not, however, altogether bleak. He perceived some good qualities among Central Americans: "physical courage, generosity, and lively intelligence."

Another notable indigenous writer with the ability to examine his own peoples with a critical eye is the Mexican Octavio Paz. In *The Labyrinth of Solitude*,[12] Paz poignantly expounds on Latin Americans' alienation from truth, already referred to by Mendieta: "We lie for pleasure. . . . The lie has a decisive importance in our everyday life. . . . The political lie has gotten imbedded in our countries almost constitutionally. . . . We move in the lie with naturalness."

Sometimes one has to experience the contrast between cultures to realize how sharply their ethical standards regarding lying, stealing, and other behavior may differ. In 1969, while I was a student in Europe, I visited London. I remember the puzzlement some of my Nicaraguan friends experienced at using the city's public buses. The conductor would ask each rider his destination. Taking the passenger's word at face value, he would charge fares accordingly. My friends, believing the system was foolish, took great delight in giving false destinations to lower their fares. The point is not so much that my friends had no qualms about cheating, but that they considered those who acted honestly as contemptible; they were naive, stupid idiots. Examples could be multiplied *ad infinitum*.

Rangel, another glaring exception to Revel's law, quotes at length from the memoirs of Francisco Miranda, a Venezuelan who traveled to the United States in 1783. When his luggage arrived in Boston, he marvelled that the customs officials let him through without even opening his trunks, "on my simple assurance that they did not contain any commercial goods." He was just discovering the contrast between a society where trust and confidence prevailed, and his native land, where distrust, cheating, and lying were the norm.

In fact, one does not need much background to discern what a casual reading of the situation in contemporary Latin America readily suggests. From the scandal of Panama's General Antonio Noriega, to the billions embezzled by high-ranking

12. Octavio Paz, *The Labyrinth of Solitude: Life and Thought in Mexico*, trans. Lysander Kemp (New York: Grove, 1962).

Mexican officers, including some former presidents, what emerges is the picture of a continent sunk in corruption and demoralization. More troublesome, the phenomenon seems to be worsening: "We are in the midst of a moral degradation unprecedented in the history of Brazil," comments Mario Amato, a leading businessman from São Paulo, Brazil. The disease seems to affect not only the ruling elite but also the entire population. Carlos Rosenbaug, a sociologist at Rio University in Brazil, speaks of the rule of "savage individualism."

Impressed by the traditional contrast between the ethical standards of North and Latin America, some observers have concluded that the different degrees of order, stability, and prosperity in their societies could be attributed largely to the moral differences. Miranda, for one, attributed the prosperity and peace of American society to the virtues of its people: diligence at work, honesty, and respect for democratic procedures. Rangel adds that an age that thrives on myths would be bewildered by an explanation as clear, as simple, as obviously true as Miranda's.

Searching for the Roots

No matter how compelling the logic of Miranda and similar authors may be, their explanations get hardly any hearing in Latin America. Rangel comments, "Anyone who still wishes to read Miranda's words today must do so in utmost privacy, for no one refers to his writing publicly any longer." (I, for one, learned about the excellent insights of my compatriot Mendieta only after I emigrated to the United States.)

The reasons for this neglect are many. Again, the lack of self-criticism that plagues social literature about Latin America often suggests that the region's moral maladies can be blamed on Western "imperialism" and, sometimes, on the corrupting influences of multinational corporations. Myrdal objected to this allegation. For him, corruption can be traced back to the traditional cultural foundations of most Third World nations. He puts it bluntly in regard to Indonesia and Africa. As a Dutch colony, Indonesia enjoyed an almost total absence of corruption, but with independence its public administration became totally corrupt in just a few years. In reference to Africa he comments, "Most of the newly independent countries in Africa are reported to have lapsed rapidly into a spreading pattern of corruption." He insists that the explanation for these changes should be sought in the "legacy of traditional society." The historical evidence, mentioned above, does indicate that Latin America's anomie has its roots in colonial times and even in many traits of pre-Columbian America.

Another common explanation, which often combines with the former one, is that corruption and lack of achievement are either by-products of poverty or defense mechanisms of peoples crushed by an oppressive social order. Lewis, Fromm, and several other authors have recognized some cultural maladies: machismo, family disruption, anomie, alcoholism, and the like. However, they almost invariably regard these as rooted in the capitalist system.

Yet in Latin America both rich and poor indulge in some anomic patterns, a fact that makes untenable the pseudo-sociological attempts at blaming moral disarray on exploitation or poverty. It should be granted, however, that seeing anomie as a defense mechanism of the poor may have different degrees of validity.

Institutional arrangements, for instance, those of the centralist tradition, do affect moral standards. Institutional constraints that bar most people from making a living by ethical and legal enterprise promote immorality. The bureaucratic rule imposed by Spain on its colonies spawned a strong temptation for Latin Americans to resort to fraud and shrewd tricks to bypass the nightmarish mess of red tape and curtailments. In time, living in the lie and outside the legal framework becomes internalized into more permanent psychological and cultural traits.

The need to emphasize the moral-cultural dimension should not be seen as an attempt to neglect sociopolitical structures, which also are important. Statecraft *can* be soulcraft. The relationship between the two has been pondered by the Western intellectual tradition. Policies can encourage or discourage virtue. Although exceptional individuals rise above institutional constraints (martyrs, for instance) most people are weak enough to bend before them.

In the high degree of anomie in Latin American societies, for instance, researchers face a phenomenon whose roots are complex enough to prevent simple answers. Sometimes anomie is fueled by discernible institutional arrangements. At other times, although overlapping with the first, intriguing racial-cultural processes intervene, as was the case of *mestizaje*, or the mixing of Europeans with people of Indian and African descent. A good examination of this phenomenon can be found in Wolf's *Sons of the Shaking Earth* and in the first chapter of Alan Riding's *Our Distant Neighbors*. The Mestizos, unable to identify with either the Spaniards (who despised them) or the Indians (who distrusted them), grew as an ethnia devoid of identity and, as such, became easy prey for anomie and a host of cultural pathologies.

Rediscovering the Religious Root

Another key element that no analyst, believer or not, can dispense with is religion as a sociocultural force that shapes values, attitudes, and moral standards. Many great secular sociologists have discovered its power through their own sociohistorical research. Christians in particular should be alert to the important role of religion because of its powerful effect on their own lives.

As there is no question that values and morals affect social life, there is no question that religion is one empirical source of values and morals, perhaps the most important. In the words of Ivan Vallier, a social scientist who has provided one of the best analyses of the role of religion in the making of Latin America, "A religion is unique among human institutions in its potential capacity for creating a general framework of meaning and universal standards of socioethical behavior."

When looking at a specific case like Latin America, research-ers working from a Christian perspective should ask what bear-ing the lack or presence of religious conversion and Christian ethics may have on the quality or type of life in the region. A Christian researcher must not forget that an exogenous ele-ment, or an indigenous social element, may have caused the misery and suffering he sees. But he should also always test the conviction that bad trees cannot bear good fruit and good trees cannot bear bad fruit (Matt. 7:16–20); that is, when he sees lawlessness, oppression, corruption, and strife prevailing in a society, he should examine the moral fabric in the hearts of the men inhabiting that unhappy land. In regard to Latin America, the researcher would have to ask to what extent a Christian cul-ture has been established on the continent. Has Latin America been truly evangelized? Have Christian values, ethics, and pat-terns of organization penetrated deeply into the social fabric of the region, or have they remained only on the surface?

Concrete analyses of Latin America in terms of these con-cerns can be collected from some of the historical and anthro-pological literature. The available information suggests that the Spaniards who conquered South America differed, in their reli-giosity and cultural traits, from the Anglos who first settled North America. Although Spain exhibited remarkable religious zeal as a nation, the men she sent to establish the first colonies included an overwhelming proportion of fortune seekers and adventurers whose ethics and religious outlook could hardly be called Christian. Many were soldiers released after the war against the Moors and, as such, had made their living from the spoils of the enemy. They were not religiously motivated family men like the North American Pilgrims who landed at Plymouth Rock or the Pennsylvania Quakers.

Although Latin America is perceived as a more spiritual, church-oriented land than the commercial, materialistic North, that perception has little basis in fact. The existing biog-raphies of many of the conquistadors and governors of the new Spanish colonies offer a telling and marked contrast with those of men leading the fortunes of the Anglo-Saxon world. Very often the former were irreligious, callous men, involved in murderous intrigues against one another. Although the religious credentials of the North American founding fathers may be ambiguous, those of many of their counterparts in the Spanish-speaking world clearly suggest a pattern of irreligiosity. Simon Bolivar, for one, was far from exhibiting the religious concerns and moral values shown by men like Abraham Lincoln.

Latin American culture, in contrast to North American, also resulted from the clash of two cultures and races. While Anglo-Saxon Americans were, in some respects, northern European transplants with a more uniform culture, Hispanic Americans were, to a large extent, a mix of Indians and Spaniards, an amalgam of Western and non-Western elements. The Indians were hastily evangelized by a few priests who achieved record-breaking mass baptisms of several thousand Indians on a daily basis and over huge expanses of land. There were reasons for the haste, but it made almost unavoidable the failure of many of the new values to permeate Latin America down to the patterns of family life and the stock of values that inform the life of the region. Pictures of Christ and images of saints may adorn many Latin homes, but their familial organization and their roles and behavior patterns are shaped more by pre-Columbian patterns or newer, non-Christian (pagan) models.

According to contemporary research, weekly participation of Catholics in the mass and monthly communion has been estimated at about 10 percent of baptized members. (The corresponding figures for the United States are over 45 percent.) Women make up an overwhelming percentage of those who participate in religious activities. Even more disturbing, religious inclinations in Latin America tend to be tied to sacramental formalism, not channeled into ethical behavior.

In Vallier's view, the church in Latin America never completed its missionary task and failed to institutionalize a religio-moral basis for social and political integration. Among the by-products are a weak value consensus and social and political instability. From his perspective, "the crux of the [region's] political problem is not to be discovered in the structure of government nor in the personalities of the leaders and officials, but in the relation between the cultural sphere and the policy."

Implications for Theology

If the failure of organized religion to permeate society and change un-Christian patterns of behavior may be one of the causes of oppression in the broadest sense (spiritual, social, and political), Christians engaged in the quest for liberation should give greater weight to the task of religious building or, simply put, evangelism and discipleship.

A Christian perspective emphatically grants culture a salient role. As a religion, Christianity is concerned not only with preaching God's salvation in Christ but also with preaching a new way of life. From the primitive church to twentieth-century missionaries, Christians have seen themselves as carrying a particular set of values, ideas, and norms. Christian activists have spent, accordingly, remarkable amounts of energy in culture building, that is, in spreading their set of values and morals.

For centuries, Christians believed in the civilizing power of the gospel, a belief whose validity history confirms. They saw preaching the gospel as a key in teaching people the way to salvation, which implied building an earthly city shaped in some specific, Christian ways. Rejecting the gospel meant rejecting the only saving truth as well as the most powerful civilizing and humanizing force.

Contemporary Christian activists, convinced of the value of their own religious principles, cannot fail to comprehend the catastrophic consequences that must follow the breakdown of religious influences on social life. From this perspective, a society that fails to follow the gospel or one in which the gospel cannot be preached stands in real darkness and oppression from which it urgently needs to be liberated. For Christians, the stakes are high. Not only some legitimate secular values (stability, prosperity, and peace) are in jeopardy when religion fails, but also the eternal destinies of men. A society in which pagan,

un-Christian ideas are eroding Christian faith and practices
ought to cause Christians more alarm than one in which many
multinational corporations are penetrating the local markets.

The incorporation of cultural-religious dimensions thus
broadens the ways in which Christians may perceive the phenomenon of oppression in different societies. They may discover that the struggle for liberation incorporates the struggle
against cultural forms that deny the ways of life and values
taught by their own religious faith and tradition. They may
define as most oppressive those societies that forcibly suppress
the preaching of the gospel or impose a pagan or secular culture
(values, norms, patterns) that radically contradicts fundamental Christian principles.

Back to a Religious Vision of Social Life

Openness to the multifold causes that may produce poverty,
oppression, and suffering in the world, especially among the
poor, may lead Christians to a more mature understanding of
the complex dynamics of social life and to the discovery of elements that the prevailing social literature often neglects. More
promising, however, is the potential this endeavor has of leading Christian activists back to their own religious sources and to
areas where religion has the most to offer.

Liberationist father Gustavo Gutiérrez wrote a book a few
years ago entitled *We Drink from Our Own Wells*.[13] The title was
probably meant to suggest that, contrary to critics of liberationism, its advocates were not drinking from Marxist or alien
waters but from their own religious tradition. It seems, however, that these protestations, like the call they issued to study
the causative factors of the social order in a scientific way, have
remained more statements of purpose than practical accom-
plishments. All too often, Christians drink from alien sources
without pausing to examine the quality and implications of the
intellectual waters from which they draw not only inspiration,

13. Gustavo Gutiérrez, *We Drink from Our Own Wells: The Spiritual Journey of a People*, trans. Matthew J. O'Connell (Maryknoll, N.Y.: Orbis, 1984).

but also categories of thought. Thus they end up endorsing views and perspectives that carry unstated presuppositions that contradict or obscure important Christian truths and often represent a truncated, incomplete view of human reality. Even more ironic, in drinking from alien waters Christians often forget that their own religious tradition holds a wealth of concerns and of specific ways of looking at things that can provide a deeper and simultaneously more realistic understanding of the roots of social and political ills.

A case in point is the sociology of institutional remedies. No doubt the analysis of social institutions and structural patterns can be illuminating. However, insofar as it sees the world as a network of institutions, and insofar as it defines most problems as sociostructural rather than cultural, it shifts attention from the human person to his social surroundings. Consequently, it implies that individuals are not the ones who should change so much as institutions. Once the institutions change, individuals will follow suit or at least the conditions for their moral improvement will have been provided. From this perspective we could find institutional cures for the illnesses that afflict both individual and society: narcissism, machismo, corruption, greed, violence, anxiety, and the rest. If we suffer from these maladies, it is because we have not been liberated enough from the social circumstances that produced them. Consequently, our hope for liberation lies not in trying to be better persons or living according to different norms as advocated, for instance, in traditional Christianity but in changing, or improving, our life conditions.

Such a view not only overlooks the many other dimensions of life that other social scientists stress, but also buys wholesale the overly sociologized image of man, according to which man is just a product of his social circumstances. If man is in a shameful state, it is because society has corrupted him. Thus, this view ignores the fundamental human realities of which the Christian tradition has been aware: man has a fallen and weak nature; he has a tendency to corrupt the best of circumstances; and he has a free will to choose between good and evil.

Moreover, the institutional remedy risks opening the door to what historian Paul Johnson calls the "ill of the century," social engineering, the assumption that human beings can be shoveled around like concrete. This assumption sustains all the coercive utopians who have populated and decimated the earth. It makes a redeeming profession of politics, and it makes secular messiahs of political leaders.

This does not mean that Christians cannot benefit from the wealth of insights provided by sound, secular sociostructural analysis; it only means that they must discern them carefully, aware of their limited and partial nature. Furthermore, when Christians look at social reality, they cannot forget to put on the lenses of their own tradition. Failure to do so may be precisely the problem. Harry Blamires has argued that Christians are no longer used to looking at social events through the lenses of their own religious categories and traditions.[14] They have largely lost, he says, "the Christian mind." A Christian may retain a different code of ethics, but as a *thinking* being he has succumbed to secularization, meaning that "he rejects the religious view of life, the view which sets all earthly issues within the context of the eternal, the view which relates all human problems social, political, cultural to the doctrinal foundations of the Christian Faith. . . ."[15]

Today's Christians will seldom trace a society's failings to the moral failings of its individuals. Even proposing that they try may provoke scorn or embarrassment among many of them. Yet, was not this concern typical of Christians meditating about the tribulations of the social world throughout most of Christendom's history?

Alexander Solzhenitsyn epitomized an important element of the religious vision of historical events in his famous but simple phrase about the reason for Russia's disasters: "Men have forgotten God; that is why all this has happened." Another Rus-

14. Harry Blamires, *The Christian Mind: How Should a Christian Think?* (Ann Arbor, Mich.: Servant, 1978).

15. Ibid., 3–4.

sian, Georgij Edelstein, expressed a similar discernment when he implied that in history sins never remain unpunished.

In the traditional religious view, closeness to or distance from God always played a role in the quality of people and in the quality of the world they make, which, of course, means far more than rates of economic development. Rejecting God was seen as rejecting the source of all goodness and wisdom and as falling under the tyranny of passions that obscure the mind and destroy body and soul. The core of the religious message was thus the call to repentance and conversion: Turn back to God! The Old Testament prophets, whom modern activists like to quote, not only denounced the establishment but also were courageous enough to denounce the sins of their own people and to call them to repentance. Will modern liberationists do the same in Latin America?

A traditional Christian belief, which the sociology of institutional remedies tends to obscure, is precisely the primacy of individual conversion, itself rooted in the doctrine of free will. The Christian does not regard man as a toy of social or economic forces, tossed in one direction or another without the mediation of his free will. Since man can choose between good and evil, he can be held accountable. This belief in the existence of individual free will is what explains Christianity's emphasis on moral exhortation. From the letters of Paul to contemporary church documents, it has been common among Christians to exhort one another to rightful behavior on the assumption that man is a being who chooses.

The religious mentality also understands the importance of love and virtue in the social order and seeks to achieve both through a long, protracted struggle in the heart of each man. Calls to repentance, conversion, piety, and penance are means whereby the religious establishment seeks to help man enter the narrow gate and, it is hoped, to transform him from a selfish, immature creature into a loving, responsible one. To these views Christians add a peculiar religious dimension. They believe that no matter how much willpower people invest in changing themselves, and, for that matter, the world, they cannot do it unless they become empowered by the Holy Spirit, whom God grants to those who turn to Christ and ask for the gift of the Spirit. The religious element is at the heart of cultural and behavioral changes; it provides the lens through which thoughtful Christians see the world.

It is ironic then that during the years when the old liberation theologians were subordinating a historic Christian vision of society to the material or the economic or the political, there has begun a renaissance of the religious vision in the study of the social world. When scholars considered religious problems in the 1960s, they tended to view them from a social perspective. Things have changed. Today, large numbers of people believe the key to understanding reality, including social reality, is religion. Once again we discover that the world has passed the old liberation theologians by.

8

Beyond Liberation Theology

After years of debate, many Catholics and non-Catholics remain puzzled over the question, Where does the Vatican stand in regard to liberation theology? Does it condemn the movement, or does it bless it?

The confusion results in large part from what appear to be inconsistent statements on the issue. The problem is complicated by attempts of partisans on both sides to interpret statements by the pope and the magisterium in ways that support their particular position. The occasional subtle nuances and puzzling ambiguities of some magisterium pronouncements have not made things easier.

This chapter is an attempt to set the record straight by examining six key documents: (1) John Paul II's opening address at Puebla, Mexico (1979); (2) the Vatican's "Instruction on Certain Aspects of the Theology of Liberation" (*Libertatis Nuntius*), published by the Sacred Congregation for the Doctrine of the Faith in 1984; (3) The Vatican's "Instruction on Christian Freedom and Liberation" (*Libertatis Conscientia*), issued by the same institution in 1986; (4) the pope's letter addressed to the Brazilian bishops (also 1986); (5) the 1988 papal encyclical

"Social Concern" (*Sollicitudo Rei Socialis*); and (6) the pope's 1991 encyclical *Centesimus Annus* ("The One Hundredth Year"), issued on the anniversary of Pope Leo XIII's encyclical *Rerum Novarum*. We will also look briefly at a 1988 papal address to the Peruvian bishops.

These documents do not exhaust the range of resources for the Catholic magisterium on liberation theology. Direct references to liberation theology appear in statements by regional episcopal bodies and various church authorities. Indirect references abound in several other church statements, including many of John Paul II's speeches. These six documents, however, represent the most direct and authoritative responses the church has issued thus far. They are explicit statements of official church views on liberation theology. Although *Sollicitudo Rei Socialis* does not fully fit this description, some reference to it is necessary, since many believe it marks a break with past Vatican teaching on issues related to the theology of liberation.

Blessing the Intent

The first official Vatican document to express explicitly the church's views on liberation theology was the 1984 "Instruction on Certain Aspects of the 'Theology of Liberation.'" By all accounts, it was very critical. It denounced the existence among liberationists of a novel interpretation "which seriously departs from the faith of the church and, in fact, actually constitutes a practical negation."

Yet, for all its forthrightness, the document stopped short of blanket condemnation of the liberation movement. In fact, the Instruction described the expression *theology of liberation* as "a thoroughly valid term: It designates a theological reflection centered on the biblical theme of liberation and freedom, and on the urgency of its practical realization." The legitimacy of the term *theology of liberation* is apparent in many other Vatican documents and papal speeches. Yet it is evident that when these documents use *theology of liberation*, what they have in view is *not* a specific school of thought or a given theological perspective already found in the marketplace of ideas. Instead, these documents understand a theology of liberation as a project, as something yet to come, something yet to be constructed. Thus the 1984 Instruction declares that "an authentic theology of liberation *will be* [emphasis added] one which is rooted in the Word of God, correctly interpreted. . . ." In another place, the Instruction states, "Thus a theology of liberation *correctly understood* [emphasis added] constitutes an invitation to theologians to deepen certain essential biblical themes. . . ."

Speaking about what it calls "the contemporary awareness of man's freedom and dignity" and "the powerful inspirations to liberation which are at work in our world," the 1986 "Instruction on Christian Freedom and Liberation" states, "The Church of Christ makes these aspirations her own, while exercising discernment in the light of the Gospel which is by its very nature a message of freedom and liberation."

In his now-famous 1986 letter to the Brazilian bishops (referred to by some liberationists as a general endorsement of this theology), the pope carefully stated his points conditionally. After reemphasizing the relevance of the Instructions of 1984 and 1986, he exhorted the bishops to frame their responses to poverty and oppression in a way that is "consistent and coherent with the teachings of the Gospel, of the living tradition and of the ongoing magisterium of the church. As long as all this is observed," he added, "we are convinced that the theology of liberation is not only timely but useful and necessary." A little later he again cautioned the bishops about the danger of reducing the salvific element of Christian liberation (which is primary) to the socio-ethical (which is derivative), which would subvert and emasculate true Christian liberation.

The Need for Cautious Discernment

It would be a grave mistake to read into the pope's letter to the Brazilian bishops any endorsement of the specific theologies of liberation advocated by the writers currently identified with the movement. An unfortunate instance of this error appears in an article in the Maryknoll magazine. There one writer claimed that publication of the pope's letter was cause for rejoicing among friends of the liberation movement. But the article conveniently neglected John Paul II's crucial conditional statements, including the expression *as long as this is observed*.

In the general context of the criticisms of liberation theology found in the aforementioned Vatican documents, all published with the explicit approval of the pope, it is clear that what the pope is doing is restating the same theme: *There is need for an authentic theology of liberation.* This contains an implication that no one should miss: *There are also unauthentic theologies of liberation.* This warning is made clear both by the pope and by the Vatican's Sacred Congregation for the Doctrine of Faith. And of course it is affirmed in many other sources.

Not surprisingly, many liberationists would have the world believe that the pope has changed his mind about those deviations of liberationism that he so sternly denounced in his opening speech at Puebla (1979), criticisms that remain apparent in his explicit endorsement of the 1984 Instruction. Claims about the pope's allegedly more sympathetic attitude toward liberation systems began to circulate following publication of the 1986 Instruction. This document, meant to complement the one of 1984, had a more positive and perhaps irenic tone than its precursor. It did not contain the same kinds of strong, direct warnings against many liberationist claims that prevailed in the 1984 publication. Instead, it embraced the yearning for liberation and proceeded to outline the Christian understanding of the liberation theme, against the background of the historical events leading up to the current situation in the world.

Yet, there is hardly a break between the two instructions. The 1986 document makes this point explicitly when it states, "Between the two documents there exists an organic relationship. They are to be read in the light of each other." A careful reading of the 1986 Instruction reveals that this claim about consistency and relationship must not be treated lightly. The 1986 document contains substantial criticisms of some of the basic tenets of liberation theology and a clear attempt to address some of the profound incompatibilities between central beliefs of the Christian tradition and doctrines advanced by secular Marxists and liberationists.

It is possible that some liberationists may soon claim that they have made the changes necessary to harmonize with the magisterium. While there is little evidence of this in the writings of better-known liberation thinkers thus far, it does raise an interesting question: *What changes are necessary to bring about true reconciliation between liberation theology and the Catholic magisterium?*

As this and other chapters in this book make clear, the Catholic Church already has issued the required denunciations of errors and doctrinal deviations. Publications and pronouncements since the 1984 Instruction suggest that the church sees the challenge ahead as a predominantly positive one. It is issuing a call to both clergy and laity to be both creative in their pursuit of liberation and faithful to the gospel. Already signs are visible that many theologians and concerned Christians are moving in the direction suggested by the church, seeking to fill in the outline of a liberation theology that offers genuine liberation from poverty, oppression, and sin.

In a speech delivered in Lima, Peru, in May of 1988, John Paul II warned one more time about mistaken forms of liberation theology that, in his words, "propose class struggle as the only viable solution." He reminded Peruvian bishops and clergy of their obligation to discern, clarify, and propose "remedies to the deviations which arise, whenever necessary."

The Vatican therefore *is* calling the church to build an authentically Christian and therefore biblical theology of liberation. But an essential part of this task is noting the more serious errors and distortions that appear in liberationist writings. Since many liberationists have denied that earlier Vatican criticisms applied to their ideas, it is important to identify some of the writers whose formulations have been challenged by Rome. After the Vatican issued its 1984 Instruction, some liberation theologians argued that the document's criticisms applied only to a very marginal current within the liberation movement, one to which they did not belong. Other liberationists argued that they never meant to teach the views the Instruction attributed to them. To judge by such reactions, the 1984 Instruction attacked a movement to which no one belonged. Except, perhaps, for Leonardo Boff and a few others, no liberation theologians were willing to admit that their ideas were the ones being repudiated.

Identifying these trouble spots in the theology of liberation is a task similar to clearing the ground before beginning to build. While it may seem negative, it is part of a constructive effort. And as the 1986 Instruction states, "Far from being outmoded, these warnings appear ever more timely and relevant."

The Christology of the Church

John Paul II made his first and most stern warning about the Christology of many liberationists during his opening address at Puebla, Mexico, in 1979. Driven perhaps by their zeal to exhort Christians to participate in political action, the writings of some liberation theologians overemphasized political concerns and thus distorted both the nature and the mission of Christ. In the pope's words,

> Now today we find in many places a phenomenon that is not new. We find "rereadings" of the Gospel that are the product of theoretical speculation rather than of authentic meditation on the Word of God. . . . In some cases people are silent about Christ's divinity. . . . Christ is alleged to be only a "prophet," a proclaimer of God's kingdom and love, but not the true Son of God. . . . In other cases people purport to depict Jesus as a political activist, as a fighter against Roman domination and the authorities, and even as someone involved in the class struggle. This conception of Christ as a political figure, a revolutionary, as the subversive from Nazareth, does not tally with the church's catechesis.[1]

1. John Paul II, "Opening Address at Puebla," in *The Pope and Revolution: John Paul II Confronts Liberation Theology*, ed. Quentin L. Quade (Washington, D.C.: Ethics and Public Policy Center, 1982), 53, 54.

The pope equally deplored some widespread distortions of Christ's redemptive mission, death, and resurrection. "Confusing the insidious pretext of Jesus' accusers with the attitude of Jesus himself which was very different, people claim that the cause of his death was the result of a political conflict: they say nothing about the Lord's willing self-surrender or even his awareness of his redemptive mission. The Gospels show clearly that for Jesus anything that would alter his mission as the Servant of Yahweh was a temptation."

The 1984 Instruction also denounced the tendency of many liberationists to reject or modify the historic Christian understanding of Christ. To cite but one example, it stated, "An exclusively political interpretation is thus given to the death of Christ. In this way, its value for salvation and the whole economy of redemption is denied."

These and similar remarks were direct responses to Christologies being developed by some liberationists. Hugo Assmann, for example, had proposed the need for new political models of Christ: "Some Christologies claim to be apolitical. . . . they offer us a Christ who has power but does not exercise it, and who never takes sides. The newer political Christologies are ways of stripping the mask off these allegedly apolitical Christs and revealing their true countenance." According to Leonardo Boff, Jesus did not consider himself the suffering servant of Isaiah 53. Jesus died for the same reason that prophets of all times have died: for upsetting the religious and political status quo. The transcendent meaning of Jesus' death was a product not so much of divine revelation as of his followers' need to explain his shameful death by crucifixion.

Jon Sobrino, a Spanish-born Jesuit priest now teaching in El Salvador, endorses the view that Jesus *became* the Son of God by obedience to the will of the heavenly Father—the ancient heresy of adoptionism. He denies that Jesus in his earthly life "was aware that he was the Son of God in the strict, metaphysical sense of the term." Sobrino also questions the practice of using the titles of Christ to support the thesis that Jesus had a messianic consciousness.

Both the Vatican and biblically faithful Protestants agree that a truly Christian theology of liberation must rest on a sound understanding of who Christ is plus a clear understanding of the nature of his redemptive mission, death, and resurrection. John Paul II summarizes the core of this understanding in the words of Peter's profession: "You are the Messiah. . . . the son of the living God" (Matt. 16:16). Apart from this fundamental truth, there is no purpose for the Christian church. Peter's proclamation is the foundation of the gospel, the good news proclaimed by Christianity. As John Paul II puts it, "The church lives by it and for it, even as the church draws from it all that it has to offer to all human beings, regardless of nation, culture, race, epoch, age, or condition." Jesus' death was no accidental by-product of his challenge to the status quo. First and foremost, it was a divinely ordained act to atone for human sin; it was the ground of our everlasting liberation from the penalty for and tyranny of sin.

This crucial point is reiterated in the 1986 Vatican Instruction on Christian Freedom and Liberation: "Through his cross and resurrection, Christ has brought about our redemption, which is liberation in the strongest sense of the word since it has freed us from the most radical evil, namely sin and the power of death." The truth about redemption is thus "the root and the rule of freedom, the foundation and the measure of all liberating action."

Christians concerned with liberation have to reckon with the testimony of Christ's own life and actions. They also must reckon with the fact that both spring from a vision of life, and of liberation, that is predominantly although not exclusively spiritual, otherworldly, and personal. John Paul II provided some examples of Christ's acts that illustrate all this: "He [Jesus] does not accept the position of those who mixed the things of God with merely political attitudes (Matthew 22:21; Mark 12:17; John 18:36). He unequivocally rejects recourse to violence. He opens his message of conversion to all, and he does not exclude even the publicans. The perspective of his mission goes much deeper."

The Doctrine of the Church

A second critical area is ecclesiology. What is the right understanding of the nature and mission of the church? John Paul II addressed this in Puebla when he linked errors in ecclesiology with a secularist understanding of the kingdom of God. He spoke of those who empty the notion of the kingdom of its full content. He criticized those who deny that we arrive "at the kingdom through faith and membership in the church" and who assert instead that citizenship in the kingdom comes rather "merely by structural change and sociopolitical involvement." He objected to liberationists who teach that the kingdom is present wherever "there is a certain kind of commitment and praxis for justice."

John Paul II also denounced the fostering by many liberationists of "an attitude of mistrust toward the institutional or official church, which is described as alienating. Over against it is set another, people's church, one which 'is born of the people' and is fleshed out in the poor."

The 1984 Instruction saw as one of the faults of the current theologies of liberation "a tendency to identify the Kingdom of God and its growth with the human liberation movement, and to make history itself the subject of its own development, as a process of the self-redemption of man by means of class struggle." Because of this view the church itself, says the Instruction, is seen *only* "as a reality interior to history, herself subject to those laws which are supposed to govern the development of history in its immanence. The church, the gift of God and mystery of faith, is emptied of any specific reality by this reductionism."

Echoing the remarks of the pope, the 1984 Instruction highlights the consequences of pitting an alleged "people's church," defined as the church of a class (the church of the oppressed), against the "institutional church." The claim that the former is born of the people contains the clear theological implication that "the ministers take their origin from the people who therefore designate ministers of their own choice in accord with the needs of their historic revolutionary mission." The result is thus "a challenge to the *sacramental and hierarchical structure* of the church, which was willed by the Lord Himself."

Although the 1984 Instruction does not mention specific theologians by name, these passages can be read as direct references to utterances of liberationists like Peruvian Gustavo Gutiérrez. In one place he wrote, "The people of God must strike roots in the exploited and the alienated classes. In fact it must rise out of those classes, out of their interests and aspirations and struggles and cultural categories." The constitutional document of Christians for Socialism, a group of radical Latin American Christians in whose birth Gutiérrez actively participated, claims that only the poor and oppressed are the true "people of God."

As a remedy for these and similar deviations, the church has called for liberationists to adhere to a sound ecclesiology. "The church is a gift of God," stated the 1984 Instruction. It does not come from the people, the proletariat, or any social class or historical agent. Rather, it comes directly from Christ. Neither is the church composed of the people in general, whether oppressed or unoppressed, struggling for justice or sitting idle. It is a community of believers, a community of faith, "the gathering together of all those who in faith look on Jesus as the author of salvation and the source of unity and peace." It consists of those who, like Peter, make the explicit profession: "You are the Christ."

As for the mission of the church, the pope defined it at Puebla as one of proclaiming and establishing among all peoples the kingdom of God. The church itself "becomes on earth the initial budding forth of that Kingdom." The 1986 Instruction declares the church's mission to be one essentially of "evangelization and salvation."

The 1986 Instruction also makes clear that these calls do not preclude, but rather include, the church's readiness to address all moral issues, including those that pertain to politics:

The church teaches the way man must follow in this world in order to enter the kingdom of God. Her teaching therefore extends to the whole moral order, and notably to the justice which must regulate human relations. . . . The church does not go beyond its mission when it speaks about the promotion of justice in human societies, nor when it condemns the forms of deviation, slavery, and oppression of which people are victims, nor when it judges certain political movements. The church may also be called to judge the value of structures, as well as the value of economic, social, and political systems . . . in terms of the extent to which they conform or do not conform to the demands of human dignity.

The 1986 Instruction does note, however, some important reservations about the church's involvement in such matters. One, repeated in the 1988 *Sollicitudo Rei Socialis*, is that the church does not side with any particular system. But as we shall see below, this apparent refusal to take sides is nuanced by the suggestion that the church may at least outline some conditions an acceptable sociopolitical system ought to meet. Proponents of Soviet-style Marxism will derive little comfort from these conditions.

Another limitation spelled out in the 1986 Instruction is that the church "should not be absorbed by preoccupations concerning the temporal order or reduced to such preoccupations." The Instruction calls the church to maintain both the unity and the distinction between evangelization and the cause of human well-being on earth, a difficult balance for which it offers no easy prescriptions. The church is also called to maintain the tension between its vocation on behalf of the weak and the downtrodden and its call to manifest universal love and concern, excluding no one. "This is the reason," the 1986 Instruction concludes, "why the church cannot express this option by means of reductive sociological and ideological categories which would make this preference a partisan choice and a source of conflict."

Competing Views of Humankind

A third critical disagreement between the Vatican and liberation theology is the doctrine of man. What is a proper understanding of human nature? Errors in this important area usually are accompanied by a defective doctrine of sin. At Puebla, the pope warned that modern versions of humanism have an inadequate view of human nature. They are frequently locked, he said, "into a strictly economic, biological, or psychological view of the human being."

The 1984 Instruction looked more closely at modern views that differ with a proper Christian view of the dignity of humankind. For example, it noted how ideologies that ignore the basic dignity of humans made in the image of God fall easily into endorsing violence. "Violence," it says, "begets violence and degrades man. . . . It mocks the dignity of man in the person of the victims, and it debases the same dignity among those who practice it."

Attempts to cure society (and individual humans) simply by trying to change social structures also result from the inadequate view of human beings as plastic beings devoid of moral potential, responsibility, and freedom, waiting to be molded by circumstances. Such thinking proceeds as if evil were just a byproduct of faulty social designs. This view, which is at the very heart of Marxism, is shared by all who, from either Left or Right, partake in what has been called "the political illusion," the belief that through sociopolitical transformations, or the imposition of new economic systems, a world of justice can be achieved.

The 1984 Instruction calls this illusion "fatal," particularly in regard to the belief that new structures will of themselves give birth to a "new man." It also calls the belief in class struggle as a road toward a classless society a myth. It adds a sobering warning: "Those who allow themselves to be caught up in the fascination with this myth should reflect on the better examples history has to offer about where it leads." The 1986 Instruction comments similarly on what it calls "the myth of revolution," or

"the illusion that the abolition of an evil situation is in itself sufficient to create a more humane society."

It is important to recognize that most authors identified as
liberation theologians have implicitly, if not explicitly, fallen
under the spell of these political illusions. They tend to find the
root of oppression and poverty in the sociopolitical realm, particularly blaming the capitalist system and what they call the
"structures of dependency." The consequences of this view are
obvious: Liberation and justice will only come through some
type of sociopolitical upheaval. "Only by eliminating private
ownership of the wealth created by human labor will we be able
to lay the foundation of a more just society," says Gutiérrez.

Juan Luis Segundo wrote that Christians must choose socialism and that this "practical political option" is, on his continent, "the focal point for the most profound and total commitments." Liberationists who act on these premises support
radical political commitment as practically the only true way of
living out one's faith. Taking sides with the oppressed against
the oppressors in the political arena is seen as a prerequisite for
being a Christian. In their view, this is the only way to love the
poor effectively. Anything less is tantamount to accepting the
oppressive order.

In short, one cannot be a Christian without also being a revolutionary committed to overthrowing "the capitalist system."
But this raises an interesting question: Can one be a Christian
merely by being a revolutionary? Many liberation theologians
have said yes, expanding Karl Rahner's idea of the "anonymous
Christian" and claiming that orthopraxis (right action) is more
important than orthodoxy (right beliefs). This approach suffers
from at least two problems. First, it undermines or obscures
what it means to be a Christian by implying that Christians are
simply those who fight for social justice. Second, it displaces
Jesus Christ with the revolution: Belief in Jesus as Lord and
Savior loses importance in the face of belief in the revolution as
a wondrous political event that will produce a new world of liberation.

As a remedy for such dangerous views, John Paul II and the two Instructions reassert the traditional Christian doctrine about the dignity of human beings and their need for a genuine, spiritual conversion to Christ. An essential element of the Christian view of man is that "the human being is the image of God and cannot be reduced to a mere fragment of nature or to an anonymous element in the human city." An inescapable implication of this claim for any theology of liberation is that humans have some inalienable personal rights, among which the right to liberty occupies an important place. Thus one indisputable guideline for judging any proposals for "liberation," says the 1986 Instruction, is this: "There can be no true liberation if from the very beginning the rights of freedom are not respected." The document extends this respect for personhood to individuals' relationships to mediating structures in society like the family, the church, and other voluntary associations. The encyclical *Sollicitudo Rei Socialis* further enriched this theme, emphasizing the value and importance of the right of economic initiative. Denying this right, the document says, "diminishes, or in practice absolutely destroys, the spirit of initiative, that is to say, the creative subjectivity of the citizen. As a consequence there arises, not so much a true equality as a 'leveling down.' In the place of creative initiative there appears passivity, dependence, and submission to the bureaucratic apparatus which, as the only 'ordering' and 'decision-making' body if not also the 'owners' of the entire totality of goods and the means of production puts everyone in a position of almost absolute dependence. . . ."

Following a consistent Catholic tradition, the 1984 and 1986 Instructions, along with 1988's *Sollicitudo*, condemn totalitarianism and collectivism because they deny the social space so essential to human freedom. Even when, in the 1988 encyclical, the pope criticizes "liberal capitalism," he does so not as an opponent of free-market economies but because, as his consultant in this matter, Rocco Buttiglione, observes, "the rule of 'big capital' over the whole economic life of a country is not conducive to true free enterprise." Echoing what seem to be the views of Latin American writers like Hernando de Soto and Mario Vargas

Llosa, Buttiglione goes on to say: "You have no idea of what capitalism is like in Latin America. Traditional economic forces suppress the free enterprise system. They have a type of hidden socialism at the service of small private groups. They bribe the government officials and have the support of the police." Of course, one must wonder why such a system should even be called capitalism. According to Buttiglione, "Never before has a Catholic Pope been so favorable to freedom of enterprise and said it is an important dimension of human freedom as such."

To go farther back, the 1984 Instruction also contains significant comments about both personal and structural change. To quote just one example, it stated, "The acute need for radical reforms of the structures which conceal poverty and which are themselves forms of violence, should not let us lose sight of the fact that the source of injustice is in the hearts of men. . . . Structures, whether they are good or bad, are the result of man's action and so are consequences more than causes." It is important to notice here that the magisterium is not so much acknowledging a reciprocity between structures and the human heart as establishing a causal connection between them that gives more weight to individual human intentions and actions.

The 1986 Instruction expands this subject even further. In one place it says, "The salvific dimension of liberation cannot be reduced to the socio-ethical dimension, which is a consequence of it." In a section titled "Primacy of Persons over Structures" it explains, "The priority given to structures and technical organization over the person and the requirements of his dignity is the expression of a materialistic anthropology and is contrary to the construction of a just social order." It also offers some important remarks about the limited capabilities of social systems to produce this order. The comments are sobering reminders to Catholic social activists not to place too much trust in institutional remedies. "It remains true," the document says, ". . . that structures established for people's good are of themselves incapable of securing and guaranteeing that good. The corruption which in certain countries affects the leaders and the state bureaucracy, and which destroy all honest social life, is a proof of this. Moral integrity is a necessary condition for the health of society."

Yet the 1986 Instruction also acknowledges that some structures may be better suited to protecting freedom than others. The very first paragraph of the document states, for example, "Freedom demands conditions of an economic, social, political, and cultural kind which make possible its full exercise." Later, in the section on the "Primacy of Persons over Structures," it affirms the right of the oppressed to take political action "through morally licit means, in order to secure structures and institutions in which their rights will be truly respected." Clearly, then, the church sees the personal and institutional dimensions as complementary; while both are necessary, primacy still belongs to the person.

Moreover, both the 1984 and the 1986 Instructions insist that personal sin lies at the root of oppression. No truly Christian theology of liberation dares ignore this point. "Sin is the greatest evil," states the 1984 Instruction, "since it strikes man in the heart of his personality. The first liberation, to which all others must make reference, is that from sin." The Instruction of 1986 expands on this theme: "Man's sin, that is to say his breaking away from God, is the radical reason for the tragedies which mark the history of freedom. . . . By sinning, man lies to himself and separates himself from his own truth. . . . Alienation from the truth of his being as a creature loved by God is the root of all other forms of alienation."

To some extent, these statements echoed older words of John Paul II: "The greatest tragedy in the world today is not the reality of any specific socio-political system, but the fact that Jesus is not known and therefore he is not loved."

The Importance of *Centesimus Annus*

Just as we were completing this book, the Vatican published John Paul II's social encyclical *Centesimus Annus*. This 1991 document argues, as Richard John Neuhaus explains, that "the poor of the world are not oppressed because of capitalism, but because of the absence of capitalism."[2] According to Father Robert Sirico, president of The Acton Institute, "[T]his encyclical constitutes the epitaph for liberation and collectivist movements in terms of any official ecclesiastical legitimacy. The 'Christian-Marxist dialogue' is dead, as even Gustavo Gutiérrez, father of liberation theology, has recently conceded."[3]

Anthropology, the Christian understanding of humanity, occupies a central role in the teaching of the encyclical. It focuses "on man's quest for a freedom that will truly satisfy the deepest yearning of the human heart." God has built the yearning for freedom into human nature. In fact, the pope argues, "Communism failed because it denied 'the truth about man.' Communism's failures were first and foremost moral failures. 'The God That Failed' was a false god whose acolytes led societies and economies into terminal crisis."

George Weigel notes the similarities between the encyclical's view of human freedom and the older view of Lord Acton: "Freedom is not the power to do what we like, but the right to do what we ought." Weigel's expansion of this point is instructive:

> True freedom, the Pope insists, is built on the basic "truth about man," which is that man has a "capacity for transcendence." Moreover, it is precisely this capacity for transcendence, man's ability to grasp the truth of things and to be grasped by that truth in ways that impel us to action that is the foundation on which societies, cultures, polities, and economies worthy of human beings can be constructed. In short . . . the answer to the false humanisms of the modern world is the true humanism that derives from Jewish and Christian understandings about human nature, human community, human history, and human destiny.[4]

2. Richard John Neuhaus in "The Pope, Liberty, and Capitalism: Essays on *Centesimus Annus*," *National Review* Special Supplement, June 24, 1991, S9.

3. Robert A. Sirico in "The Pope, Liberty, and Capitalism," S13.

4. George Weigel in "The Pope, Liberty, and Capitalism," S16.

The document does more than attack Marxism; it also criticizes the modern welfare state. "By intervening directly and
depriving society of its responsibility," the document argues,
"the social assistance state leads to a loss of human energies and
an inordinate increase of public agencies which are dominated
more by bureaucratic ways of thinking than by concern for
serving their clients and which are accompanied by an enormous increase in spending. In fact, it would appear that needs
are best understood and satisfied by people who are closest to
them and who act as neighbors to those in need."[5]

The encyclical makes much of the important but often overlooked distinction between societies (voluntary human associations like the church and the family) and the state, the organization of humans that claims a monopoly on the use of coercive
power. Among the inalienable rights of the human person, the
pope insists, "is the 'natural human right' to form private associations" (#7). The modern megastate threatens these voluntary societies in many ways, each of which must be resisted.
Modern statists also undermine the operations of a market system.

> Economic activity, especially the activity of a market economy,
> cannot be conducted in an institutional, juridical or political
> vacuum.[6] On the contrary, it presupposes sure guarantees of
> individual freedom and private property as well as a stable cur-
> rency and efficient public services. Hence the principal task of
> the state is to guarantee this security so that those who work
> and produce can enjoy the fruits of their labors and thus feel
> encouraged to work efficiently and honestly. The absence of
> stability, together with the corruption of public officials and
> the spread of improper sources of growing rich and of easy

5. The argument in *Centesimus Annus*, sect. 48, echoes similar criticisms in three
books by Ronald H. Nash: *Freedom, Justice and the State* (Lanham, Md.: University Press
of America, 1980); *Social Justice and the Christian Church* (Lanham, Md.: University
Press of America, 1992 [1st ed., 1983]); and *Poverty and Wealth: Why Socialism Has
Failed* (Richardson, Tex.: Probe, 1992 [1st ed., 1986]).

6. Compare the similarity of this position to central themes of this book's discussion
of capitalism.

profits deriving from illegal or purely speculative activities, constitutes one of the chief obstacles to development and to the economic order.[7]

According to the pope, "the social nature of man is not completely fulfilled in the state, but is realized in various intermediary groups, beginning with the family and including economic, social, political and cultural groups which stem from human nature itself and have their own autonomy, always with a view to the common good."[8]

Weigel summarizes the pivotal role *Centesimus Annus* will have in all future discussions of Catholic social theory:

> Americans who have dismissed modern Catholic social teaching as an irrelevant irritant because of the Church's assumed allergy to the free economy will have to go back to the intellectual drawing boards in the light of *Centesimus Annus*. So, too, will those brethren (on the Left) who have tried to position John Paul II as the last hope of socialism with a human face. A free economy disciplined by democratic politics and a moral culture built on the truth about man: that is the authoritative Catholic vision of the right-ordering of society at the end of the twentieth century. The Catholic "answer" to the failures of Marxism and the excesses of Manchesterian liberalism is in and the answer is democratic capitalism, rightly understood.[9]

Proponents of the old liberation theology can draw absolutely no comfort from the words of *Centesimus Annus*; nor can any Marxist or socialist or Catholic/Protestant statist. The social, political, and economic dimension of the pope's vision of a new liberation theology can be summarized in two words: *democratic capitalism*. The spiritual side of the new liberation theology is synonymous not with the assorted concessions to theological liberalism and apostasy so prevalent among the old

---

7. *Centesimus Annus*, sect. 48.

8. From *Centesimus Annus*, sect. 13. Compare to similar views in Nash, *Freedom, Justice and the State*, chap. 1, and Nash, *Social Justice and the Christian Church*, chap. 2.

9. Weigel in "The Pope, Liberty, and Capitalism," S16.

liberation theologians but with the Christian church's historic focus on the salvation and transformation God offers sinful humans through the redemptive death and resurrection of the God-man, Jesus Christ.

Going Beyond Liberation Theology

In its discussion of liberation theology, the Catholic Church has stressed the need to uphold and protect three basic truths: the truth about Christ, the truth about the church, and the truth about man. Taken together, these three truths constitute, in the words of the 1984 Instruction, the "indispensable pillars" of true liberation. No true theology of liberation can be developed if any of these truths is not respected in its entirety.

Within these parameters, there still remains a vast field where all members of the church are called to contribute in a creative way. As Neuhaus puts it in *The Catholic Moment*, what the Vatican has done in its documents on liberation theology is far more significant than a simple assault on liberation theology: "The Instruction (of 1986) is a formidable intellectual and theological exercise in setting forth the Christian understanding of a free and just social order. . . . It represents a continuing development in Roman Catholic social teaching and is an ecumenical and interreligious invitation to join in a new conversation about connections between transcendent hope and temporal responsibilities."[10]

The 1984 and 1986 Instructions and *Centesimus Annus* offer reflection on two key issues that surely will capture growing attention as Christians move beyond the older expressions of liberation theology. One is the rich theme of freedom. A theology of liberation should also be a theology of freedom. When it takes this assignment seriously, liberation theology will study the social and political conditions that restrict fundamental human liberties; it will identify and support the conditions that support such liberties. The other issue is the call to build what

10. Richard John Neuhaus, *The Catholic Moment* (San Francisco: Harper and Row, 1987), 214.

the Latin American bishops gathered at Puebla in 1979 called "the Civilization of Love" and the 1986 Instruction called "The Civilization of Work." "The solution of most of the serious problems related to poverty," claims the latter document, "is to be found in the promotion of a true civilization of work."

Such a statement obviously needs further elaboration. Nonetheless, the growing use of the term *civilization* is suggestive, for it draws attention to the importance of building or rebuilding a Christian culture as one condition for the attainment of a truly liberated society. It also invites a shift in the emphasis from structures to culture, from the all-absorbing concern with institutions to the relatively neglected concern with values, ideas, and morals. It challenges Christians with the difficult but significant task of creating a new ethos, capable of shaping the structures of society in ways harmonious with human dignity.

While the struggle against unjust social structures is legitimate, creating a new Latin America is no simple matter of trading one political and economic ideology for another. Ultimately it will depend on millions of Latin Americans becoming new persons who work to create new communities. This can only happen as individual persons are renewed in their hearts and values by the power of Jesus Christ.

The documents we have studied reveal a consistent but carefully nuanced position on liberation theology that can be summarized in these words: *The Roman Catholic Church neither rejects nor blesses liberation theology in toto. However, it does reject a specific type of liberation theology that has been developed by certain theologians. At the same time, the church blesses some of the goals of the liberation movement and thus finds nothing wrong in principle with attempts to develop a theology of liberation.*

In other words, the Roman Catholic Church is saying: *We need a truly Christian theology of liberation.*

Many versions of liberation theology proposed thus far contain serious deficiencies. The church must move beyond these defective or false liberation systems and build one that is thoroughly consistent with Christ's mandate to care for the poor and the oppressed in ways that are faithful to the Scriptures and to the needs of the poor themselves. It is time to move beyond the liberation theologies that have been proposed to this point and build one that is less dependent on questionable ideologies. It is time to begin constructing a new liberation theology that will provide true liberation from poverty, oppression, and sin.

Select Bibliography

The following bibliography contains a representative sampling of works that expound, defend, or criticize liberation theology. No attempt has been made to provide a complete bibliography. Most of the cited works refer to additional sources.

Works Supportive of the Old Liberation Theology

Alves, Rubem. *A Theology of Human Hope.* Washington, D.C.: Corpus, 1969.

Anderson, Gerald H., and Thomas F. Stransky, eds. *Mission Trends No. 4: Liberation Theologies in North America and Europe.* Grand Rapids: Eerdmans, 1978.

Assmann, Hugo. *A Theology for a Nomad Church.* Translated by Paul Burns. Maryknoll, N.Y.: Orbis, 1976.

Berryman, Philip. *Liberation Theology.* Philadelphia: Temple University Press, 1987.

_____. *The Religious Roots of Rebellion: Christians in Central American Revolutions.* Maryknoll, N.Y.: Orbis, 1984.

Bigo, Pierre, *The Church and Third World Revolution.* Translated by Jeanne Marie Lyons. Maryknoll, N.Y.: Orbis, 1977.

Boff, Clodovis, and Leonardo Boff. *Salvation and Liberation: In Search of a Balance between Faith and Politics.* Translated by Robert R. Barr. Maryknoll, N.Y.: Orbis, 1984.

Boff, Leonardo. *Jesus Christ Liberator: A Critical Christology for Our Time*. Translated by Patrick Hughes. Maryknoll, N.Y.: Orbis, 1978.

_____. *Liberating Grace*. Translated by John Drury. Maryknoll, N.Y.: Orbis, 1979.

Brown, Robert McAfee. *Gustavo Gutiérrez*. Makers of Contemporary Theology series. Atlanta: John Knox, 1981.

Croatto, J. Severino. *Exodus: A Hermeneutics of Freedom*. Maryknoll, N.Y.: Orbis, 1981.

Dussel, Enrique. *Ethics and the Theology of Liberation*. Translated by John Drury. Maryknoll, N.Y.: Orbis, 1978.

_____. *Philosophy of Liberation*. Translated by Aquilina Martinez and Christine Morkovsky. Maryknoll, N.Y.: Orbis, 1985.

Eagleson, John, ed. *Christians and Socialism*. Translated by John Drury. Maryknoll, N.Y.: Orbis, 1975.

Eagleson, John, and Philip Scharper, eds. *Puebla and Beyond: Documentation and Commentary*. Maryknoll, N.Y.: Orbis, 1979.

Ellacuria, Ignacio. *Freedom Made Flesh: The Mission of Christ and His Church*. Translated by John Drury. Maryknoll, N.Y.: Orbis, 1976.

Gutiérrez, Gustavo. *The Power of the Poor in History*. Translated by Robert R. Barr. Maryknoll, N.Y.: Orbis, 1983.

_____. *A Theology of Liberation:* Translated by Caridad Inda and John Eagleson. Maryknoll, N.Y.: Orbis, 1973.

_____. *We Drink from Our Own Wells: The Spiritual Journey of a People*. Translated by Matthew J. O'Connell. Maryknoll, N.Y.: Orbis, 1984.

Gutiérrez, Gustavo, and Richard Schaull. *Liberation and Change*. Atlanta: John Knox, 1977.

Hennelly, Alfred T. *Theologies in Conflict: The Challenge of Juan Luis Segundo*. Maryknoll, N.Y.: Orbis, 1979.

Herzog, Frederick. *Liberation Theology.* New York: Seabury, 1972.

Herzog, Frederick, ed. *Theology of the Liberating Word.* Nashville: Abingdon, 1970.

Houtart, François, and Andre Rousseau. *The Church and Revolution.* Maryknoll, N.Y.: Orbis, 1971.

Lehmann, Paul. *The Transfiguration of Politics.* New York: Harper and Row, 1975.

MacEoin, Gary. *Revolution Next Door: Latin America in the 1970s.* Maryknoll, N.Y.: Orbis, 1981.

McFadden, Thomas, ed. *Liberation, Revolution and Freedom.* New York: Seabury, 1975.

Míguez-Bonino, José. *Christians and Marxists.* Grand Rapids: Eerdmans, 1976.

_____. *Doing Theology in a Revolutionary Situation.* Philadelphia: Fortress, 1975.

_____. *Toward a Christian Political Ethics.* Philadelphia: Fortress, 1983.

Miranda, José Porfirio. *Communism in the Bible.* Maryknoll, N.Y.: Orbis, 1982.

_____. *Marx Against the Marxists. The Christian Humanism of Karl Marx.* Translated by John Drury. Maryknoll: N.Y.: Orbis, 1980.

_____. *Marx and the Bible: A Critique of the Philosophy of Oppression.* Translated by John Eagleson. Maryknoll, N.Y.: Orbis, 1974.

Ogden, Schubert M. *Faith and Freedom: Toward a Theory of Liberation.* Nashville: Abingdon, 1979.

Petulla, Joseph. *Christian Political Theology: A Marxian Guide.* Maryknoll: Orbis, 1972.

Ruether, Rosemary Radford. *Liberation Theology.* New York: Paulist, 1973.

Schaull, Richard. *Encounter with Revolution.* New York: Association, 1955.

_____. *Heralds of a New Reformation.* Maryknoll, N.Y.: Orbis, 1984.

Segundo, Juan Luis. *The Liberation of Theology.* Translated by John Drury. Maryknoll, N.Y.: Orbis, 1976.

_____. *Theology for Artisans of a New Humanity.* 5 vols. Maryknoll: Orbis, 1973–74.

Sobrino, Jon. *Christology at the Crossroads: A Latin American Approach.* Translated by John Drury. Maryknoll, N.Y.: Orbis, 1978.

_____. *The True Church and the Poor.* Translated by Matthew J. O'Connell. Maryknoll, N.Y.: Orbis, 1984.

Sobrino, Jon, and Juan Hernández Pico. *Theology of Christian Solidarity.* Translated by Philip Berryman. Maryknoll, N.Y.: Orbis, 1985.

Torres, Sergio, and John Eagleson. *Theology in the Americas.* Maryknoll, N.Y.: Orbis, 1976.

Torres, Sergio, and Virginia Fabella, eds. *The Emergent Gospel: Theology from the Underside of History.* Maryknoll, N.Y.: Orbis, 1978.

Wallis, Jim. *Agenda for a Biblical People.* New York: Harper and Row, 1976.

Works That Criticize the Old Liberation Theology and That Defend a New Liberation Theology

Hundley, Raymond. *Radical Liberation Theology: An Evangelical Response.* Wilmore, Ky.: Bristol, 1987.

Lopez Trujillo, Alfonso. *Liberation or Revolution?* Huntington, Ind.: Our Sunday Visitor, Inc., 1977.

Nash, Ronald H. *Poverty and Wealth: Why Socialism Has Failed.* Richardson, Tex.: Probe, 1992.

_____. *Social Justice and the Christian Church.* Lanham, Md.: University Press of America, 1992.

Nash, Ronald H., ed. *Liberation Theology.* Grand Rapids: Baker, 1988.

Norman, Edward. *Christianity and World Order.* New York: Oxford University Press, 1979.

Novak, Michael, *The Spirit of Democratic Capitalism.* New York: Simon and Schuster, 1982.

_____. *Will It Liberate? Questions about Liberation Theology.* Mahwah, N.J.: Paulist, 1986.

Novak, Michael, ed. *Capitalism and Socialism: A Theological Inquiry.* Washington, D.C.: American Enterprise Institute, 1979.

_____. *Liberation North, Liberation South.* Washington, D.C.: American Enterprise Institute, 1981.

Nuñez, Emilio A. *Liberation Theology.* Chicago: Moody, 1985.

Quade, Quentin L., ed. *The Pope and Revolution: John Paul II Confronts Liberation Theology.* Washington, D.C.: Ethics and Public Policy Center, 1982.

Schall, James V. *Liberation Theology in Latin America.* San Francisco: Ignatius, 1982.

Other Works

Armerding, Carl E., ed. *Evangelicals and Liberation.* Phillipsburg, N.J.: Presbyterian and Reformed, 1977.

Berger, Peter L. *Pyramids of Sacrifice: Political Ethics and Social Change.* New York: Basic, 1974.

Gilder, George. *Wealth and Poverty,* New York: Basic, 1981.

Hayek, Friedrich A. *The Road to Serfdom.* Chicago: University of Chicago Press, 1944.

Kirk, Andrew. *Liberation Theology: An Evangelical View from the Third World.* Atlanta: John Knox, 1979.

_____. *Theology Encounters Revolution.* Leicester: InterVarsity, 1980.

McCann, Dennis P. *Christian Realism and Liberation Theology: Practical Theologies in Creative Conflict.* Maryknoll, N.Y.: Orbis, 1981.

McGovern, Arthur F. *Liberation Theology and Its Critics: Towards an Assessment.* Maryknoll, N.Y.: Orbis, 1989.

_____. *Marxism: An American Christian Perspective.* Maryknoll, N.Y.: Orbis, 1980.

Nash, Ronald H. *Freedom, Justice and the State.* Lanham, Md.: University Press of America, 1980.

_____. "The Economics of Justice." *Christianity Today* 23: (1979).

_____. "Three Kinds of Individualism." *The Intercollegiate Review* 12 (1976).

Neuhaus, Richard John. *The Catholic Moment.* San Francisco. Harper and Row, 1987.

Sigmund, Paul. *Liberation Theology at the Crossroads.* New York: Oxford University Press, 1989.

Index